H ... NTS A ...

A G ... TI AND SU ... HE HOME

By

HENRI ROSE

Illustrations by

ANNIE LE FAOU

A LITTLE GUIDE IN COLOUR

PAUL HAMLYN

London . New York . Sydney . Toronto

CONTENTS

Published by The Hamlyn Publishing Group Ltd
Hamlyn House, The Centre, Feltham, Middlesex
By arrangement with Western Printing Hachette International, Genève

First Published 1967
Reprinted 1968, 1971, 1972
ISBN 0 601 07989 2
Printed in Italy by Arnoldo Mondadori Editore, Verona

INDOOR PLANTS

Origins of Indoor Plants.

The whole of the earth's surface, with the exception of the deserts, ice caps, and those mountains which have permanent glaciers, is covered with plant life. The plants themselves vary widely according to the climatic zones in which they live. Within the zones, too, very different types of vegetation are found. In the *intertropical zone*, between the tropics of Cancer (23½°N) and Capricorn (23½°S), three types of vegetation are to be found. A basic knowledge of these zones and conditions would prove to be useful, when considering house plants.

1. Tropical forest, often called virgin forest, consists almost entirely of evergreen plants. Because of the constant temperature and the high rainfall, all these plants —tall trees, creepers, some of which may reach the very top of the forest giants, shrubs and small herbaceous plants — are in growth throughout the whole year.

2. Tropical deciduous forests, bordering on the tropical evergreen forest, the most extensive of which are in Africa, consist mainly of deciduous trees. In these regions there are two very distinct seasons: the dry season, a period in which the plants enter a resting state and lose their leaves, and the rainy season during which all the plants begin to grow again and put on a covering of leaves.

3. Savanna consists of vast areas of land covered mostly by tall herbaceous plants, with isolated deciduous trees or shrubs growing among them; vegetation in savanna regions is also subject to dry seasons and rainy seasons, and the dry season is even hotter than in the tropical deciduous forest.

These types of vegetation, differing according to the

TROPICAL AND SEMI-TROPICAL ZONES

TEMPERATE ZONES

POLAR ZONES

natural conditions in the zones, also vary with altitude, type of soil, prevailing winds, and nearness to the sea.

It is mainly the first two regions described above, the tropical evergreen and deciduous forests, that provide most of the plants used for decorating the home; the requirements of these plants depend generally on their place of origin.

The *temperate zones* extend geographically from the tropics to the polar circles (66½°N and 66½°S), but, when dealing with plants, further distinction is made into the *warm temperate zone* and the *cold temperate zone*. It is only the warm zone, extending approximately from the tropics to the 40th parallels north and south, which provides our ornamental indoor plants. The cold zone plants are unsuitable for indoor life. In the warm temperate zone vegetation consists of both evergreen and deciduous plants, in proportions varying with the area and altitude; in some regions it consists only of stands of conifers. The temperate regions also contain the grasslands, where the soil is parched in the summer and where the rainfall is low, even during the rainy season. A very typical arid grassland zone exists in Mexico, which, in spite of its harsh climate, supports various plants, including some of the cacti. These plants, which present a particularly rich variety, are now much appreciated for their decorative qualities.

THE REQUIREMENTS OF PLANTS

Like all living things, plants need certain elements which are indispensable for their development: air, warmth, water, light and soil. If any one of these is lacking, the development of the plant will be disturbed and it will eventually die.

Air

The whole of a plant participates in the process of respiration, but this takes place mainly in the leaves. A plant's 'lungs' consist of cells situated under the epidermis, or outer covering, of the leaves, communicating with the exterior through small pores, the stomata, (singular: stoma), through which air is absorbed and carbon dioxide or oxygen are discharged. The air is broken down, with the action of sunlight, into oxygen and carbon dioxide. The plant gives off the oxygen, retaining the carbon dioxide which it breaks down further into several substances essential for tissue growth. During the night, the gaseous exchanges are reversed: the plant retains the oxygen and gives off the carbon dioxide—the normal pattern of animal respiration. Transpiration takes place through special stomata; in this process, the plant eliminates the excess water which it has taken up through its roots, and which is carried up to the leaves through numerous minute tubes.

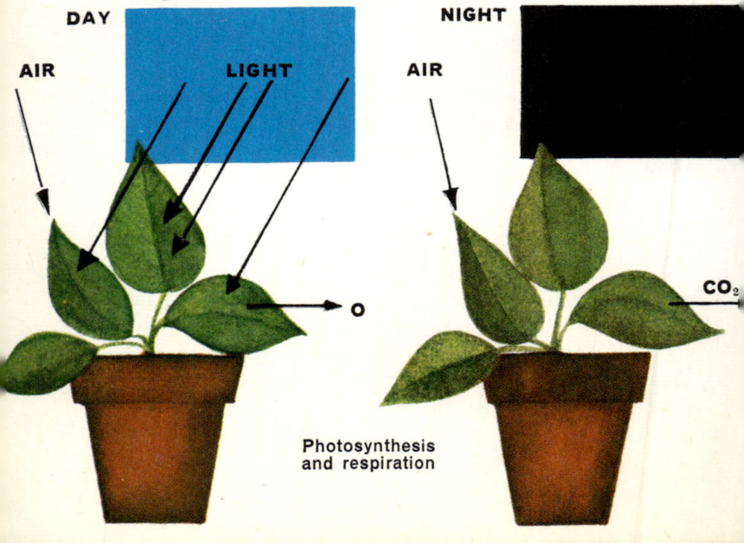

Photosynthesis and respiration

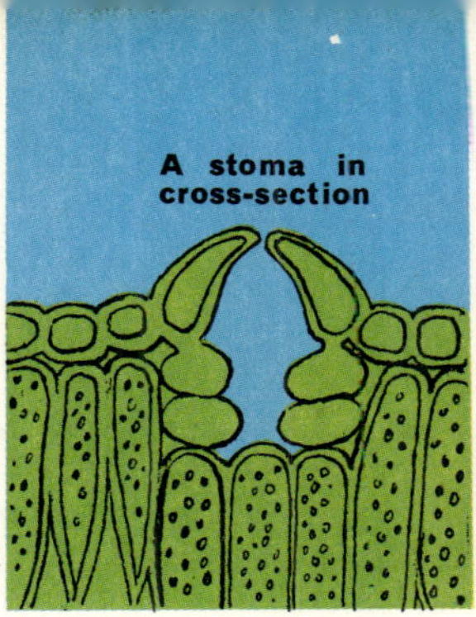

Warmth

The temperature required by a plant varies according to its natural habitat, and so to cultivate it correctly one must find out its place of origin. Plants requiring a high temperature will soon die in a place of low temperature, which slows down their natural processes, preventing normal growth and development. Similarly, plants from a cold region, if subjected to high temperatures, will grow too rapidly; the tissues become soft and weak, the plant wilts and finally dies. These two examples explain why the cultivation of plants in sometimes unsuccessful indoors, where the temperature may not always be correct.

Water

Plants need water. They take it from the soil, absorbing it through the *root hairs*. This water has dissolved minerals from the soil and so contains numerous elements; it is carried by the plant right up to the leaves, where it undergoes various changes, to form the substances needed for the building of new tissues. Rainwater, which is always well aerated and free from lime, is the best to use for watering plants; unfortunately, it is not always possible to collect it. Very hard water containing lime should be avoided; it is harmful to some plants, especially to ferns.

Soil

Plants are classified as *calcifugous* (lime-hating) and *calcicolous* (lime tolerant), according to the type of ground on which they grow. Calcifugous plants grow where the soil contains no lime or chalk; they should be potted in a lime-free compost containing a generous supply of peat, and should not be watered with hard water containing lime. Lime tolerant plants, on the other hand, can be grown in soils containing lime such as the John Innes composts or similar mixtures. But whatever the type of soil, it is essential that it should be light and loose enough to permit the free circulation of air between the soil particles, as well as the proper drainage of excess water. It is sometimes useful to add sand to make the soil more permeable. Thick-leaved plants in particular need a very permeable soil and cannot tolerate water-logged conditions.

calcifugous plants	{ 1/2 heath-mould 1/2 compost	+	peat (retains moisture)
calcicolous plants	{ 1/3 fresh-earth 2/3 mould	+	river sand

Light

Light is essential to the life of plants, but not all plants require it in the same intensities. Some, such as the cacti and the spurges, thrive on strong sunlight and grow on open ground. Others, such as the ferns,

which occur naturally in undergrowth, require diffused sunlight. Indoors, where natural light is sometimes limited, plants should be placed where it is most plentiful, but without forgetting their preferences. They should never be put directly behind glass, as on an inside window-sill, where there is a risk of causing burns on the leaves. A net curtain between the window and the plants is sufficient to protect the plants, without reducing the amount of light needed for healthy growth.

Care and Attention

All plants cultivated indoors demand careful attention if good results are to be obtained. As already explained, their requirements will depend on their place of origin. We will consider two types of plants: 1. those which come from regions where there is continuous plant growth (these regions provide most plants used for decorating the home), and which are called *green plants*; 2. those which come from regions with a dry climate, where growth is limited to only a part of the year, such as *thick-leaved plants* and *bulb-bearing plants*.

Plants with Continuous Growth

All these plants have persistent leaves. If they are to be maintained in a state of continuous growth, the earth in their pots must be kept moist: it must be watered often to prevent the leaves from wilting. Some plants, for example the ferns, which are very sensitive to a 'dry spell', lose their leaves permanently, while in others which are more resistant only the lowest leaves turn yellow and drop off. But, while not allowing the soil to dry out, it is just as important not to go to the other extreme of watering it every day or standing the pot on a saucer which is constantly topped up with water. This very often smothers the roots, and causes the earth to decompose and become very acid, so that the plant withers and finally dies because its roots cannot tolerate such conditions. With a little experience, it is easy to see when a plant needs watering; the surface of the soil becomes lighter in colour, and the pot gives a hollow note if tapped and will be much lighter when picked up.

The frequency of waterings should vary with the seasons, and according to the strength of the plant. In summer, when plants are most active and their loss of moisture is highest, and when the evaporation of water from the soil is also higher, waterings should be more frequent than in winter, when there is a slowing-down of growth. A plant in poor health will absorb less water than one in a good state of growth and development. Water should be given, whether in one or more waterings, until no more is retained by the soil and the excess starts to drain away through the hole in the bottom of the pot. In this way, the whole mass of earth is uniformly moistened, making the soil suitable for the healthy growth of the roots. The next watering should be made when the surface of the soil is dry, not leaving it until the whole pot has dried out. Small amounts of water given every day are bad for the plants. After some time the earth at the bottom of the pot dries out as the small quantities will only moisten the top inch or two; the roots are then no longer fed, and the plant soon wilts and usually dies.

If watering has been neglected and a plant does wilt, the best way to revive it is to stand the pot in a vessel full of water for about an hour. Because most green plants are cultivated in compost containing peat or leaf mould, it is very difficult to moisten the whole mass of dried earth in a pot by ordinary watering. In addition, by being soaked in this way the plant regains its essential element very rapidly; in many cases, the leaves quickly become stiff again and the damage done is limited.

The *temperature of the water* given to plants should preferably be the temperature prevailing in their place of origin. The dry air in houses and flats, especially those that are centrally heated, is usually not suitable for plants, for in these conditions it is almost impos-

sible to achieve the level of humidity found in greenhouses. To augment the natural moisture in the air, it is essential to leave vessels containing water on the radiators or in front of fires (special 'saturators' can be obtained for this purpose), which should always be kept topped up. In rooms with a very dry atmosphere, it is possible to create a microclimate: the pots are placed on a water-filled bed of fine gravel in a dish or plastic tray about 2 inches deep. In this way, the bottom of the pot is not standing in the water but evaporation from it maintains a moderate level of humidity around the plants.
The *temperature* which should be maintained depends similarly on the place of origin of the plants. The most suitable temperature in each case is given in the description of the plants on the following pages. The situations in which continuously growing plants are placed can be very important. Sometimes a plant

will just not be 'happy' where it has been put and will wither. If it is moved to a new spot, it often regains its strength; for the same reason, rather than saying that a plant like this 'isn't holding its own', one should try to find the best situation in which to keep the plant.
Another essential operation is cleaning the leaves. Dust collects on the skin and blocks up the pores, preventing proper respiration and evaporation. From time to time, the leaves should be washed with a soft sponge. This washing can also be used to treat the plant against parasites by adding a suitable insecticide to the water, taking care to follow the manufacturers' instructions, to avoid any danger of burning the leaves with a too highly concentrated solution.

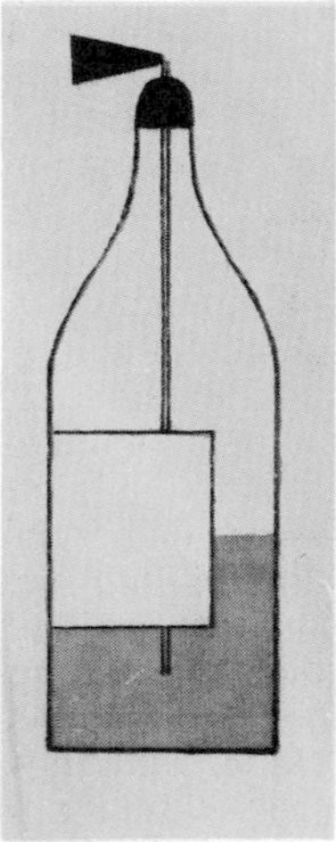

Plants with Interrupted Growth

This category includes nearly all thick-leaved plants. They originate from regions where periods of rest alternate with periods of growth, and to obtain the best results from their cultivation the natural rhythm of their development must be considered. In our climate, the active period corresponds to summer and the resting period to winter. The attention required by these plants is different from that given to green plants. Watering during the active period is required less frequently than in green plants. It is even preferable to wait until the earth in the pot has dried up before giving more water, rather than to keep the soil constantly wet. In winter, when growth is very slow, watering should be stopped almost completely, especially if the plants are kept at the correct temperature. Some succulents, however, are exceptions to this rule: all the members of the Crassulaceae, the aloes, *Gasteria*, *Haworthia*, and two cacti (*Epiphyllum* and *Phyllocactus*), none of which have a period of total rest, and so should be kept slightly moist. Some of these even flower in the winter, for example the Kalanchoe, *Epiphyllum* and a few of the aloes. But the other cacti should never be watered during the winter period, to ensure good blooms when the normal period of growth starts again.

PROPAGATION

Cuttings

Some cuttings will root only with the use of special techniques, but it is still well within the ability of the amateur to propagate many plants by this method without very much trouble. When taking a cutting from the stem, a section should be chosen which has three or four buds, and a clean cut made just below the last bud. This stem is then inserted in a pot

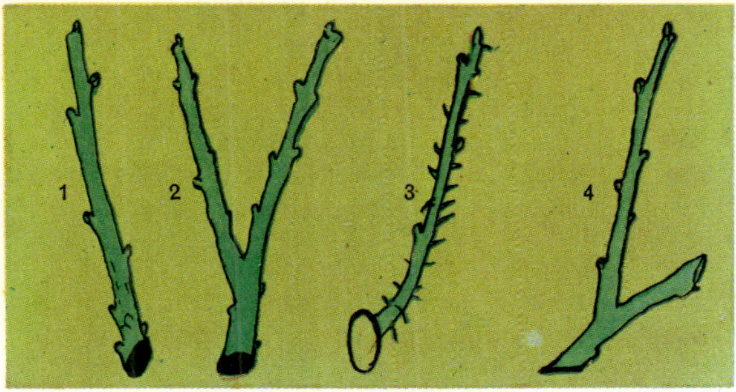

Cuttings of leafless stems

1 and 2: simple stems **3: heel cutting** **4: new shoot cut with part of old stem**

containing a free-draining compost, which must be kept moist. After some time, a swelling forms at the base of the cutting, which then gives off young roots. To encourage rooting and to prevent the cutting from withering, a fairly high humidity should be maintained for the first week or two.

Leaf cuttings are possible only with some plants, and each species requires different methods. With *Saintpaulia* and *Peperomia*, the leaf-stalk is cut in pieces $2\frac{1}{2}-3\frac{1}{2}$ inches long, which are planted vertically about 1 inch deep. In the case of the *Cyperus*, the stalk is cut 1 inch from the cluster of leaves, which are thus shortened by more than half; the cutting is placed in water, where it soon gives off roots and

Preparing and cutting of a stem in leaf

young shoots; the cutting is then ready for repotting. The Rose-laurel can also be propagated by cuttings placed in water, but in this case the cutting should be a small branch.

The best time of the year for making cuttings of this type is from April to May. When taking leaf cuttings from succulents, the leaves should not be cut but divided. They should be left to dry for about eight days, then shallowly planted or just placed on the surface of the soil. Cuttings of cacti and *Euphorbiaceae* should also be left to dry until the wound has healed completely, then planted in very sandy compost. They should not be watered until three or four days after planting, and then only very lightly at first. The best time to make cuttings of cacti and other succulents is May to June, when the temperature is favourable for the striking and growth of cuttings.

Offsets

This is a very simple method of propagation. The small bulbs produced from fully mature bulbs form a clump at the base of the plant, the clump is divided up, and each part is potted just like a normal plant. Only plants which give off numerous offsets, like *Aspidistra* and *Sansevieria*, can be propagated in this way.

Seeds

A germinating seed needs warmth, moisture, air, careful attention and daily observation. Propagation by seeds is not only confined to professionals, who have special equipment, but in the case of most plants, this method is well within the reach of the amateur, without the use of elaborate equipment.

In most cases a seed-pan or small pot filled with John Innes Seed Compost should be used. Place a piece of crock over the drainage hole of the pot or pan and

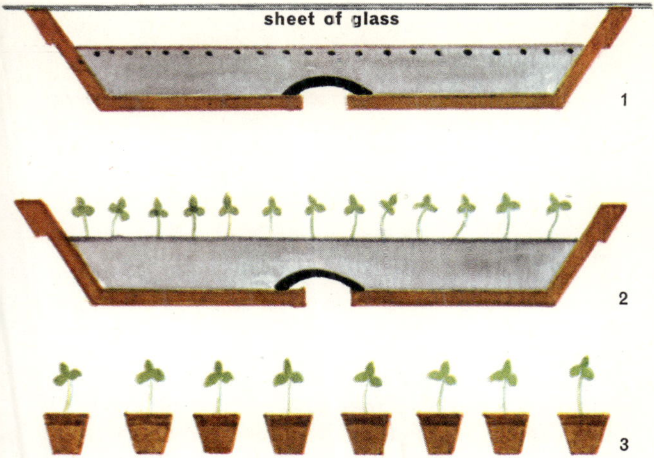

fill it with moist compost to within about ½ inch of the rim, firming it lightly to a smooth level surface. Sow the seeds as thinly and evenly as possible, and cover them lightly with finely sifted compost. As a general rule, the seeds should be covered with a depth of earth equal to their own thickness, but very small seeds should be lightly pressed into the surface of the compost and not covered at all. After sowing, water them, using a very fine rose for sprinkling. Alternatively, the pot can be stood to three-quarters of its depth in a bowl of water until the water seeps upwards to the surface. This is recommended for very fine seeds. After watering by one or the other of these methods, the pot should be covered with a sheet of glass and put in a place with a constant temperature, preferably 65-70° F, to obtain rapid germination. Now the soil must be kept moist.
The glass is removed as soon as the seedlings ap-

pear, and the pot placed in the light. When the young plants have two or three leaves, they should be potted individually in pots of suitable size (avoid choosing one which is too big), then watered and put in a warm place to encourage rooting. The best time for sowing seed is March to April, when the days are getting longer and the light is stronger, both of which are helpful for the healthy growth of the young plants.

REPOTTING

When they are cultivated in pots, plants are provided with a rather small amount of earth, which limits their supply of nutrients. For this reason, they have to be repotted occasionally to give them access to fresh soil. Not all plants have to be repotted every year. Types which develop quickly, like *Ficus* and *Chlorophytum*, need a more frequent supply of new soil, while palms and *Cycas* can easily wait two years. Cacti are less demanding still and can go even longer without repotting. It is quite easy to see when a plant needs repotting. When all the nutrient substances in the soil are exhausted, the leaves become smaller, the root system runs right through the whole mass of soil and soon absorbs all the moisture in it, so that it dries up more quickly and has to be watered more often.

Select a pot with a diameter 1-1½ inches greater than the old one, put a piece of crock over the drainage hole, then add a little compost; the depth of this should be such that when the plant is put on top with its old clump of earth, the top of the clump is still about ½ inch below the rim of the pot. Now pour fresh earth into the space between the pot and the plant, and press it down gently with the fingers or a piece of wood, depending on the depth of the pot. Finally, cover the surface of the old soil with a thin

Repotting

layer of new compost. As soon as the repotting is completed, the plant should be well watered, so that both the old and the new soil are thoroughly moistened. Never repot a plant with its clump of earth completely dry. To ensure rapid re-establishment after repotting, keep the plant in a warm moist atmosphere for a few days. When a plant is unhealthy, the cause will often be that the roots are in a bad condition, in which case, repotting can sometimes be a remedy, but now a smaller, not a larger, pot then the old one should be used. When cacti are repotted, unlike green plants, they should not be watered immediately but only after two or three days. The best time for repotting is in March or April, when growth is speeding up and the weather is more mild. Waterings with a fertilizer solution play an important part, complementary to that of repotting, by providing a steady supply of nutrients. Applications can be given about every two weeks during the period of active growth. They should never be given when the earth in the pot is dry, and careful attention should be paid to the manufacturer's instructions.

DESCRIPTIONS OF THE PLANTS

ACANTHACEAE

APHELANDRA leopoldii. Brazil. The leaves are 6 – 7 inches long, and have yellowish-white lines running along the smaller veins. The yellow flowers grow in a terminal spike, subtended by large bracts of a similar colour which turn reddish with age. The bracts are more persistent than the flowers and themselves form a decorative part of the plant. This species is cultivated for both its flowers and its foliage, but has the slight disadvantage of losing some of its leaves after flowering. It is often used for temporary decoration.

AMARYLLIDACEAE

CLIVIA miniata. Southern Africa. A strong indoor plant which flowers every year in the spring. The flowers, which grow in an umbel, are vermilion. The leaves are linear, dark green, and grow to 16 - 20 inches in a fan-like pattern. The various varieties of this species differ only in the size of their flowers and leaves, the colour of the flowers being the same for all. The suckers, which appear at the base of the plant, can be separated off when they are strong enough and have a few rootlets growing from the neck.

APHELANDRA LEOPOLDII

CLIVIA MINIATA

BRASSAIA ACTINOPHYLLA

APOCYNACEAE

NERIUM oleander (Oleander). Southern Europe. This is a plant which does not require very high temperatures (from 41 – 47° F), and can be used for decoration in cold spots. It forms bushy clumps with branches 2 – 3 feet long. The leaves are dark green and grow in a whorl. The flowers, which may be white, pink, red or yellow, simple or double, grow in a terminal spike; they bloom in July to August. During the summer months, the Laurel-rose can be put in the open air. On the Côte d'Azur it is cultivated in open beds. There is a variety of this species with leaves variegated with white. The sap of the Laurel-rose contains a dangerous poison.

NERIUM OLEANDER

ARALIACEAE

BRASSAIA actinophylla (Umbrella Tree). Australia. This species has only recently been cultivated as an indoor plant, and really deserves to be more widely appreciated. The single stem carries long-stalked, digitate leaves 12 – 20 inches long, composed of three to five leaflets when young, and from seven to twelve in mature plants; these leaflets are oblong, 8 – 10 inches long, and are themselves carried on stalks 2 – 3 inches long which radiate from the tip of the main stalk. On the upper third of the bright green leaflets, situated in a slight depression on the side of the blade, are two or three small horny spines about ½ inch long. The arrangement of the leaflets gives the whole leaf the appearance of an umbrella. When it has grown to a large size, this plant can be used to decorate large rooms or halls where the temperature varies between 59–64° F.

DIZIGOTHECA elegantissima (Elegant Aralia). New Hebrides. This very decorative species has a single stem, carrying compound leaves of seven to eleven very narrow leaflets, toothed on the edges and of a reddish-green colour. The leaf-stalk is very slender, marbled in light yellow and dark green. If it is to thrive and not lose its leaves, this plant must have a temperature in the region of 64° F and high humidity. To obtain a more decorative effect, two or three plants can be grouped together in the same stand. Propagation is by cuttings, and is rather difficult to accomplish indoors.

FATZHEDERA lizei. A hybrid, obtained by crossing *Fatsia japonica* with the common Ivy. Its leaves are identical in shape to those of *Fatsia*, but are smaller. The stems do not twine like those of the common Ivy and are also thicker, but they can be trained on a frame as they continue to grow. Like its two parent species, this plant does not require a high temperature during winter months; 41-47° F is sufficiently warm. For this reason it is often used for decorating cold places. *Fatzhedera lizei* can safely be put in the

DIZIGOTHECA
ELEGANTISSIMA

FATZHEDERA LIZEI

open during the summer if it is kept out of strong sunlight, and will grow well in shady situations indoors. There is a variety with leaves variegated with white which has to have plenty of light in the winter. It is a little less hardy than the standard plant, but more decorative.

FATSIA japonica (Japanese Aralia). Japan. A very strong indoor plant, usually with only one stem. The big palmate leaves are a beautiful shiny green. Almost hardy in southern England, it is used in the decoration of places where the temperature stays between 47 – 50° F. The variety called *moseri*, with leaves variegated with yellow, is a stockier form but is nevertheless more frail. Properly cultivated, *Aralia* can grow to 5 feet; when it reaches this height and is well covered with leaves, it is most impressive. *Fatsia* cannot stand the direct rays of the sun, which cause the leaves to yellow and drop off.

HEDERA helix (Common Ivy). A very widespread woodland plant, Ivy is often cultivated for indoor decoration. It is very hardy, and lends itself to various arrangements either as a climbing or a hanging plant. Ivy can stand low temperatures, but also does quite well in a warm room. Moreover, it will

FATSIA JAPONICA

HEDERA HELIX

grow satisfactorily in places with only poor light. There are several varieties obtained by selection, which have leaves of plain green, or variegated with white or yellow. During the summer months these varieties can be used for decorating balconies. Ivy is propagated by cuttings, preferably in August, and by layering at any time of the year.

ARACEAE

AGLAONEMA commutatum. Malaysia. This plant grows to a height of 12 – 20 inches, and has a rootstock giving off numerous suckers. The oval, lance-shaped leaves are a shiny dark green, with grey markings along the main veins. The variegated Aglaonema requires a high temperature and a high level of humidity, but will not suffer if one watering is missed. It will adapt to poor light, although in these conditions the grey markings will be less pronounced. It is particularly suitable for growing in a vase with a nutrient solution. The flowers are white, with a spathe which does not open very wide.

AGLAONEMA COMMUTATUM

ANTHURIUM SCHERZERIANUM

AGLAONEMA robelinii. Malaysia. A species with wide leaves, the margins and centre of which are grey-green and enclose two irregular silvery bands.

AGLAONEMA pictum. Sumatra. Leaves a delicate green with grey markings.

These three species are all propagated either by stem cuttings or by offsets.

AGLAONEMA PICTUM

ANTHURIUM scherzerianum (Flamingo Flower). Costa Rica. A stemless plant which forms clumps 12 – 16 inches high. The oblong, lance-shaped leaves are dark green, with stalks slightly swollen at the base. The inflorescence, consisting of a spathe and a spadix, may be in various shades of pink or red, sometimes white spotted with red. The spathe persists on the plant for a long time and the spadix, which in this species is pink, grows in a spiral, so that together they produce an attractive effect. If it is to grow to a good size, this plant requires a temperature from 59–64° F and a lot of light, although it cannot stand direct sunlight. The inflorescence can be used as a cut flower and will stay fresh for more than three weeks.

DIEFFENBACHIA picta. Brazil. A beautiful plant with a single stem carrying large oblong leaves, green with silvery markings on the upper surface. It is rather delicate indoors and needs plenty of watering, a temperature of 59–64° F, a moist atmosphere and very good light, without which the leaves yellow and fall. Several varieties exist; *fournieri* has leaves irregularly mottled with yellowish patches; *bausei* is a stocky variety with delicate green leaves with white markings and a green border. The variety *arvida* is a compact plant with dark green leaves variegated with creamy white, needing a temperature of only 50–54° F. These plants need plenty of watering during the summer.

MONSTERA deliciosa (Swiss Cheese Plant). Mexico. This curiously attractive plant has recently become very popular. It has large leaves with curious perforations on each side of the main vein and deeply cut margins. Young cultivated plants have smaller leaves which are often entire. *Monstera deliciosa* is fairly tolerant as regards temperature, but demands very good light and a high level of humidity. Adult plants develop thick stems that are not very long, and are suitable for decorating

DIEFFENBACHIA PICTA

The plant grows quite slowly, and needs plenty of light, high humidity and an average temperature of 60° F. The stem gives off adventitious roots, which should be trained back into the soil in the pot. Another species, *Philodendron houllettianum*, with similarly cut leaves, can stand lower temperatures.

large rooms. The stem gives off numerous adventitious roots, which are most useful to the plant if they are trained into the pot. This plant sometimes produces an edible, highly scented fruit, from which it gets its name.

PHILODENDRON elegans. Tropical America. A climbing plant which should be trained up a stake. The stem is thick, with few branches, and the long-stalked leaves are cut almost to the midrib into narrow strips.

PHILODENDRON scandens (Climbing Philodendron). Mexico. This very sturdy climbing plant, with pliable, branched stems, should be trained on a frame or on columns. The heart-shaped leaves are shiny and coloured a beautiful shade of green. The Climbing Philodendron must by watered frequently and preferably placed in a humid atmosphere; it also requires plenty of light, although it cannot stand the direct rays of the sun. It will grow perfectly well in poor light, but in these conditions the leaves will be smaller. Propagation is easy, whether by stem cuttings or by layering. The inflorescence of Philodendrons consists of a spadix and a rolled spathe; this particular species rarely flowers under cultivation.

PHILODENDRON selloum. Brazil. This differs from the other Philodendrons in having a stem which is almost non-existent in the young plant and continues to grow very slowly, giving the plant a characteristic appearance. The leaves are very large and are cut halfway to the midrib into

PHILODENDRON SCANDENS

PHILODENDRON SELLOUM

strips, which are themselves lobed in outline. When the leaves fall, the long stalks leave round white scars on the stem, which add to the attractiveness of the plant. The stem gives off thick adventitious roots which sometimes reach a considerable size. *Philodendron selloum* is a sturdy, resilient plant, particularly suitable for decorating large rooms where the temperature may fall to 55 – 60° F.

SCINDAPSUS pictus. Java. A climbing plant with numerous stems giving off adventitious roots, wich allow it to be attached to a support. The leaves are asymmetrically heart-shaped, of a brilliant dark green with many silvery-white spots. This species can be trained on a frame, or it can be grown as a hanging plant. It is propagated easily by stem cuttings. A smaller species, *Scindapsus aureus*, has fewer stems and leaves variegated with yellow, which need plenty of light if they are to keep this coloration. It can be grown only as a climbing plant; its stems are thicker and need to be trained on a support. Both species require an average temperature of 65° F and a humid atmosphere.

SPATHIPHYLLUM wallisii. Colombia, Venezuela. This plant is not often used for indoor decoration, although it deserves more appreciation. It forms attractive groups 12 - 16 inches high, with bright green, oval, lance-shaped leaves, from which grow numerous white flowers with spadix and upright spathe; the flowers are very persistent, so that

SYNGONIUM AURITUM

the plant makes a show for a large part of the year. *Spathiphyllum wallisii* is a sturdy plant which grows well in a temperature of 60 – 65° F and with good light. It should be watered throughout the year but less frequently in winter, although the plant can and should be kept in growth through this season. *Spathiphyllum floribundum* also carries a lot of flowers, but the spathe, which is white, is upright only at first, curving as the plant grows older. Propagation, which is by offsets, should be carried out in spring.

SYNGONIUM auritum. Mexico. A climbing plant with very rapid growth. The leaves are divided into three or five segments with yellowish-green veins. The plant's stem gives off numerous adventitious roots and needs to be trained on a support. This species is attractive only when young, for as the stem grows longer it loses its basal leaves; it is preferable to prune the plant by taking cuttings, which are easily propagated. *Syngonium albo lineatum* has brilliant green leaves divided into five to seven segments, with white midrib and lateral veins. *Syngonium green gold* is generally similar, but its leaves are spotted with yellow. All these plants must have plenty of light, without being exposed to the direct rays of the sun, frequent watering, a humid atmosphere and a minimum winter temperature of 60° F.

ZANTEDESCHIA aethiopica. Africa. This plant is better known as the Arum Lily. The leaves are light green, lance-shaped in outline, and are carried on stalks 16–24 inches long. The inflorescence consists of a spotless white trumpet-shaped spathe and a golden yellow spadix. It grows from a rhizome, which starts its growth in February or March; the flower-like inflorescences appear from May onwards. In autumn, when the leaves yellow, waterings should be spaced out gradually to take the rhizomes into their winter resting state. During the period of active growth, on the other hand, the plant should be watered more frequently. Propagation is carried out easily, by division of the rhizome. *Zantedeschia albomaculata* has leaves spotted with white, also white spathes. *Zantedeschia elliottiana* is distinguished by a golden-yellow spathe and transparent white spots scattered all over its leaves.

ZANTEDESCHIA AETHIOPICA

BEGONIACEAE

BEGONIA rex. Himalayas. The original plant is not often seen, but the numerous varieties are

BEGONIA REX

very widely cultivated. They form very attractive groups with their heart-shaped leaves and very varied colouring. There are small flowers which appear in the autumn, but these plants are mainly cultivated for their foliage. If they are exposed to too much sun, the leaves fade and may be burned; they thrive best in a well-lit situation, shaded from the direct rays of the sun, where the temperature is from 60 – 65° F. During the growing period, from March to the end of October, the plant should be watered frequently. In winter, waterings should be reduced and the temperature should now be from 55 – 60° F to ensure the state of half rest which the plant must have, until it starts growing vigorously again in the spring. Applications of dilute liquid fertilizer during the growing period help the development of the leaves. *Begonia rex* can be propagated easily, by leaf cuttings or by division of the rhizome.

AECHMEA FASCIATA

BROMELIACEAE

AECHMEA fasciata. Brazil. All the members of this family are stemless plants with the leaves arranged in a somewhat open rosette like its tropical member, the pineapple. In *Aechmea fasciata*, the leaves are upright, with the upper part curved back; they are stiff, grooved and fringed with spines, and are marbled on both sides with irregularly spaced whitish-green transverse bands. The inflorescence grows from the centre of the plant. It ends in an elongated head bearing small blue flowers (which

ˌECHMEA
ULGENS

become pink as they fade) which grow from the base of pink bracts fringed with small spines. The flowers are short-lived, but the thin, dry bracts persist for several months during which the plant is still very decorative.

AECHMEA fulgens. Guyana. Compared with *Aechmea fasciata*, the leaves of this species are less stiff and form a more open rosette. They are green, and fringed with many small, soft spines. The inflorescence forms a compound spike with small blue-petalled flowers, growing from an inflated red calyx; the flowers are short-lived but the calyx persists for several months. The variety *discolour* is generally similar, but the leaves are a brilliant green above and purple-violet on the under surface. These plants do well indoors, but need plenty of light if their inflorescences are to open fully. The rosette disappears some months after the flowering, but by this time it has given off several offsets, which can be used to propagate the plant.

AREGELIA carolinae. Brazil. This plant has a very open rosette of light green leaves, 12 inches long and about 1½ inches wide, with toothed margins. The flowers form a head in the centre of the plant, and are not very attractive. But at the time the flowers appear, the bases of the central leaves take on a bright red colour, giving a particularly striking effect. The variety *tricolour* has leaves variegated with

AREGELIA CAROLINAE

yellowish-white lengthwise bands; these also redden at the base at the time of flowering. This is a very attractive variety. The sheathing arrangement of the leaves helps water to accumulate at the centre of the plant or at the base of the leaves; this water does no harm during the summer, but in winter it is better to prevent it from collecting, because it could cause rotting, especially if the plant is in a cold spot. *Aregelia carolinae* is propagated by separating off shoots; it should be kept at a temperature of 60 – 65° F.

AREGELIA spectabilis. Brazil. The leaves are 10-14 inches long, upright and finely toothed on the margins; they are slightly leathery, green with bright red tips, the under surface with transverse ash-grey bands of irregular width on a greenish-brown ground. The small flowers, white with violet spots, form a head at the centre of the plant. This is a very sturdy species which has the added advantage that its rosette persists in good condition for more than a year after the flowering; it also gives off shoots.

AREGELIA SPECTABILIS

AREGELIA PRINCEPS

AREGELIA princeps. Brazil. The leaves are shining green, fringed with fine soft spines, and take on a bright red colour at the base at the time the flowers appear.

BILLBERGIA nutans. Brazil. The leaves are 10–12 inches long, sheathing in the lower part and curved back in the upper part, with small, widely spaced spines on the edges. The flowers have green petals with violet-blue borders, and are curved back and rolled up towards the outside; they begin to fade on the second day after flowering. Each flower, however, is accompanied by a pink bract which persists for five or six days, and gives the slender, hanging inflorescence the appearance of a bunch of pink flowers.

BILLBERGIA saundersii. Brazil. This plant forms a wider rosette than the last species. The leaves are wider and covered all over with white, pink and brown spots. The foliage of this species is the most attractive of the whole genus, and it really deserves to be used more widely than it has been.

CRYPTANTHUS zonatus. Brazil. A dwarf plant forming an open

CRYPTANTHUS ZONATUS

rosette, with leaves 6–8 inches long, of a reddish-green with grey crosswise stripes. The wavy leaves are leathery, and have a border of small spines. White flowers appear at the centre of the plant, but, as in all of the Bromeliaceae, they are very short-lived.

CRYPTANTHUS bivittatus. Brazil. Basically similar to the last species, this plant has dark green leaves with two ivory-white lengthwise bands.

Both these species are hardy indoor plants which are quite happy in fairly poor light, and can stand being left without watering for quite long periods. The shoots appear near the centre of the plant and can be separated very easily.

NIDULARIUM striatum. Brazil. One of the most attractive species, with an open rosette of upright leaves, 10 – 12 inches long, fringed with small whitish spines. Initially pale green with white lengthwise lines in the middle, the leaves turn yellow with age. It is a plant which requires plenty of light. The inflorescence, which emerges only a little way from the

NIDULARIUM STRIATUM

CRYPTANTHUS BIVITTATUS

centre of the plant, is accompanied by green, pink-tipped bract-like leaves.

NIDULARIUM rutilans. Brazil. The leaves are wider and also wider spread than those of the last species, and coloured light green with dark green patches. The pink flowers, with their bright red bracteal leaves, are carried on an inflorescence protruding only slightly from the centre of the plant. Propagation is by separation of shoots, when the shoots have grown quite strong.

NIDULARIUM RUTILANS

TILLANDSIA DIANTHOIDEA

TILLANDSIA dianthoidea. Central America. This is a plant with an unusual existence. In its native habitat it is essentially epiphytic — growing on other plants, but not taking nourishment from them. It can also be cultivated in the same way and it is not unusual to see specimens forming quite big clumps, considering the large number of small rosettes which have developed. Each rosette is 3–5 inches high, with grey leaves 1½–2 inches long, from the centre of which grows an inflorescence 4 inches long, with blue flowers and pink bracts.

In summer, these plants should be sprayed with water frequently and if possible kept in a humid atmosphere; fresh air and plenty of light are also good for them. In winter, they should be put in a temperate spot with good light, and watered lightly from time to time.

TILLANDSIA lindeniana. Ecuador. This plant is also epiphytic in its native country. To obtain a large specimen, it should be grown in a very light soil mixture. The leaves, 8–10 inches long and roughly an inch wide, are green with reddish-brown lines; they form a very attractive rosette from the centre of which grows an inflorescence in the form of a flattened spike. The large violet-blue flowers are short-lived, but open one after the other on alternating sides of the spike. The colour of the spike persists after the flowers have faded, prolonging the decorative effect of the plant.

TILLANDSIA LINDENIANA

VRIESEA splendens. Guyana. This is the bromelid most cultivated for sale by florists, as much for its hardiness as its decorative value. It has leaves 12-16 inches long, upright and curved back slightly at the tip, green with blackish transverse bands on both sides. The inflorescence is 16–20 inches high, ending in a flattened lance-shaped spike formed by the bright red overlapping bracts. The tubular yellow flowers, which appear at the base of these

VRIESEA SPLENDENS

bracts, open on both sides of the spike at the same time. The spike persists for a long time but loses its attractive bright red colour as it grows older. *Vriesea splendens* is a plant which requires a situation where the light is very good.

COMMELINACEAE

CALLISIA elegans. Mexico. This very attractive little creeper, which has been in cultivation for only a few years, is equally decorative as a pot plant or in the garden. It is similar to the *Tradescantia* but is smaller and the leaves, which are green above with yellowish lengthwise lines and slightly pinkish below, grow closer together. If it is put in strong sunlight, the leaves are much more colourful and the plant stays rather short. The inflorescence is an upright spike growing at the ends of the stems, with small white, three-petalled flowers of short duration. Numerous adventitious roots grow from the stems, and propagation by cuttings is easy.

CALLISIA ELEGANS

RHOEO
DISCOLOR

RHOEO discolor. Mexico. A plant closely related to the *Tradescantia* but with a very different appearance. It forms a thick stem 4 – 8 inches high, with lance-shaped leaves 6 – 8 inches long, dark green above and violet-purple below. The small white flowers grow together in two bracts which form a small cup, inserted into the base of the leaves. The variety *vittata* is distinguished by leaves variegated with yellowish lengthwise lines. The stem nearly always gives off adventitious roots, and it is very easy to propagate the plant by cuttings. Both species also readily produce shoots at the base which can be used for propagation. They must be given plenty of light, especially *vittata*, which will otherwise lose its leaf markings. The soil should always be kept moist, and in winter the temperature must be between 55 – 60° F.

SETCREASEA purpurea. Mexico. This plant has been introduced only recently, and really deserves to be seen more widely. The short, slightly creeping stems are sheathed in lance-shaped leaves 6 inches long and about 1 ¼ inches wide, with long white hairs on both surfaces.

SETCREASEA
PURPUREA

The leaves are purplish-green above and violet below, with longitudinal veins of a deeper colour. If placed in good light, even in the sun, the colours intensify and become a violet-purple, sometimes with a bluish sheen. The plant thrives in good light and does not grow too quickly. The flowers, which form a short, long-stalked inflorescence, appear readily but are short-lived. They are about ⅜ inch across, with three purplish-pink petals, accompanied by two large bracts.

TRADESCANTIA ALBIFLORA

TRADESCANTIA albiflora. South America. A well-known house plant, this plant has branched creeping stems, with stalkless, sheathing leaves. The leaves are a shining green, but there are other forms of the plant with leaves variegated with white or yellow. They can be used as hanging indoor plants. This species can stand slightly shady situations and does not suffer much if one watering is missed. The stems give off numerous adventitious roots, which makes it very easy to take cuttings of the branches. As they grow old, the stems tend to lose their basal leaves; for this reason it is preferable to propagate new plants periodically by taking cuttings. This species rarely flowers; when it does the flowers are white. In winter, the plant must be sheltered from frost.

TRADESCANTIA
BLOSSFELDIANA

TRADESCANTIA blossfeldiana. Brazil. This recently introduced species has a stem with long trailing roots, and short thick branches covered with white hairs. The thick, purplish-green leaves are also covered on both sides with these hairs. The purplish-white flowers grow abundantly in clusters. Individual flowers last only one day, but new ones continue to replace them for several weeks. Another form, *variegata*. has leaves with lengthwise markings of yellowish-white and pale green. This plant forms attractive groups, but cannot be used as a hanging decoration like the other *Tradescantias*. It is easily propagated by cuttings. It is very resistant, and will put up with poor light and tolerate variations in temperature, as long as it does not drop below 45 – 50° F.

ZEBRINA pendula. Mexico. This plant is also known as *Tradescantia zebrina*. It is generally similar to *Tradescantia albiflora*, but the leaves are larger and coloured differently; they are entirely purple on the under surface, while above they are streaked along their

ZEBRINA PENDULA

length with silvery-white and dark green lines. The pink flowers are short-lived. This is a hanging plant like *Tradescantia albiflora*, but it needs plenty of light to retain the attractive colouring of its leaves, although it should not be exposed for too long to the direct rays of the sun.

ZEBRINA purpusii. Mexico. The leaves of this species are wider, reddish-green above and darker below; it is also a little hardier than *Zebrina pendula*.

Both species are easily propagated by stem cuttings.

ZEBRINA PURPUSII

CYCADACEAE

CYCAS revoluta. China, Japan. For hardiness, elegance and strength, this plant deserves to be

CYCAS REVOLUTA

among the most popular species. It looks rather like a little palm tree with a swollen trunk, topped with a crown of leaves from 20 – 40 inches long, depending on the strength of the stock. These leaves consist of narrow leaflets growing very close together; the leaflets are dark green, leathery, curled at the margins and tipped with a sharp point, and may persist for several years. This plant requires a temperature of 50 – 55° F, and lends itself well to the decoration of halls. It rarely flowers indoors, although this sometimes occurs with old plants; the inflorescence is more curious than beautiful. *Cycas revoluta* is a very slow-growing plant.

CYPERACEAE

CYPERUS alternifolius (Alternate-leaved Cyperus). Madagascar. This semi-aquatic plant is very widely used for decorating aquariums and in the home. It forms thick clumps with round stems 24 – 39 inches long, between which appear the small and rather uninteresting inflorescences. This type of plant needs a constant level of humidity; it is also a good idea to place the pot in a saucer of water. This Cyperus is propagated either by offsets or by cuttings of leaf rosettes placed in water to take root. The variety *gracilis* is a less important plant which does not grow taller than 20 inches; its stems and leaves are smaller. Often wrongly called *Papyrus*, this species differs from the last in having a larger rosette composed of very fine, drooping leaves, and a stem that is triangular in cross-section.

SCIRPUS cernuus. South America. Also an aquatic plant, this one forms clumps of leaves 8 – 12 inches long; the leaves are a beautiful green, thread-like, and grow upright with the upper part hanging down.

CYPERUS ALTERNIFOLIUS

SCIRPUS CERNUUS

The small, rather uninteresting flowers grow in small spikes carried on stalks similar in appearance to the leaves. This plant cannot stand missing even one watering, and it is recommended to keep the pot standing permanently in a saucer of water. It can be used as a hanging plant, either in a suspended basket or standing on a high shelf or on a pedestal, etc. It is propagated easily by offsets. *Scirpus cernuus* is also suitable for decorating terrariums, but in these the plant should be grown rather high up, so that the leaves are not trailing in the water.

EUPHORBIACEAE

CODIAEUM variegatum. Malaya. A very decorative plant with richly coloured leaves. In the original plant, the leaves are oblong, linear, more or less deeply lobed, and vary in size in the different varieties. They are always colourfully variegated in various shades of green, yellow, red and pink. The markings are

CODIAEUM VARIEGATUM

more or less regular, sometimes arranged in lines along the veins. This beautiful plant needs very special attention. It must have a temperature of 65 – 70° F and a moist atmosphere. In dry air, as in heated rooms, the leaves will fall. To prevent this happening, a microclimate can be created; the pot is put on a bed of stones in a saucer of water, so that the pot is not actually standing in the water, but evaporation keeps the atmosphere moist. Changes in temperature should also be avoided.

GESNERIACEAE

COLUMNEA crassifolia. Mexico. A plant with thick, half-woody stems. The fleshy leaves are linear, lance-shaped and opposite, dark green above and below a paler green with red veins. The tubular, red flowers, 3 – 4 inches long, grow from the leaf axils.

COLUMNEA gloriosa. Costa Rica. A plant with slender hanging stems. The leaves are small and green, covered, like the stems, with reddish hairs. The variety *superba* has reddish leaves. This variety is used as a hanging plant, which is particularly attractive when it

COLUMN
GLORIO

blooms, when each stem carries about ten tubular flowers 3 – 4 inches long, bright red with yellow throats. All these plants need a moist, warm atmosphere, about 60° F, good light (but not direct sunlight), plenty of watering in the summer, rather less in winter; good blooms can be obtained if these conditions are provided.

SAINTPAULIA ionantha (African Violet). Tropical East Africa. Widely popular now for some years, this delightful little plant has the advantage that it is almost permanently in flower when grown indoors. The thick, oval, blunt leaves, 4–5 inches long, grow in a roundish clump; they are dark green above and below are sometimes purple, depending on the variety. Both the leaves and their stalks are covered with little hairs. The flowers of the species are a velvety violet, with a boss of golden-yellow anthers in the centre. There are now numerous varieties, all of them very pretty, with single, or double, white, pink or mauve flowers. To get good growth, the plant should be put in the light, but not under the direct rays of the sun, and watered regularly without wetting the leaves. Propagation is by leaf cuttings, which develop readily, although it takes several months before the new plant is ready to bloom.

SAINTPAULIA IONANTHA

GRAMINEAE

OPLISMENUS hirtellus variegatus. Northern Central America. A useful little plant in a number of ways. The stems are slender, creeping with the tips growing upwards; the leaves are sheathing, lance-shaped, undulate, 2–2½ inches long, and a delicate green with white lines, sometimes touched with pink if they are exposed to sun-

OPLISMENUS
HIRTELLUS VARIEGATUS

light. The flowers are small and grow in a spike; they are of no great decorative value. This plant, with its creeping stems, is suitable either as a hanging decoration or for edging the staging in a greenhouse or conservatory, where it will grow profusely. The stems give off numerous branches, which in turn give off adventitious roots at each node. Direct sunlight does it no harm at all, and in winter it must also have plenty of light. The numerous adventitious roots make propagation by cuttings very easy.

LILIACEAE

AGAPANTHUS umbellatus. North Africa. A rhizome-bearing plant with radical leaves 24 – 30 inches long, reflexed at the tip and arranged in straight rows on opposite sides of the stem. The flower stem is 30 – 39 inches tall, and carries at the tip an umbel of from thirty to fifty blue flowers. The plant is almost hardy in the southern half of England, but should be taken in for the winter further north. Plants in pots require very little water during the winter. In April waterings should become more frequent,

AGAPANTHUS
UMBELLATUS

and the plant should be put on a balcony or somewhere with plenty of air and light; to get good blooms in July-August, it will also need a lot of watering. There is a variety of *Agapanthus* with white flowers.

ASPARAGUS PLUMOSUS

ASPARAGUS plumosus. South Africa. Everyone knows this very delicate foliage which is used to decorate almost every bunch of flowers. It comes from a plant with numerous modified branches called cladodes, which look like little leaves, and give it a feathery appearance. It is widely grown by commercial growers for supplying to florists' shops. It can be harmed by direct sunlight, and it requires a temperature around 60° F. If it is kept in subdued light, the leaves stay a deeper shade of green. The form with climbing stems can be trained on a frame, with very decorative effect. It should be well watered in summer, moderately in winter. Propagation is by cuttings from young side shoots. The variety *nanus* forms lower and tighter plants, but has the same requirements.

ASPARAGUS SPRENGERI

ASPARAGUS sprengeri. Natal. Unlike the last species, this plant gives off spiky hanging branches, with cladodes about an inch long growing in whorls; these carry small pinkish-white flowers, which produce fruits the size of a pea, green at first but turning red when ripe. This is a very 'hungry' plant which rapidly uses up the nutrients in the soil; dressings of liquid fertilizer will help to ensure good growth. The very abundant roots form spherical swellings which grow to the size of a cherry and very rapidly fill the pot. When this happens, the plant should be repotted to provide it with the additional nourishment it needs. The arrangement of the stems and branches makes this plant suitable for growing either in a hanging basket or on a pot-stand, in a situation with plenty of light but shaded from the direct rays of the sun.

ASPIDISTRA lurida (Aspidistra). China, Japan. Although not so fashionable an indoor plant today as it once was, this is certainly one

ASPIDISTRA LURIDA

of the toughest of all. It can be left in a poorly lighted spot and not watered for several days, and will still continue to grow. If it does get good light, plenty of water and attention to its leaves, it soon grows to a considerable size. The leaves, which grow on stalks from a rhizome, are 20–24 inches tall, with oblong lance-shaped blades of a dark, shining green. The flowers are more unusual than decorative. They appear on the surface of the soil, and have a purplish colour. The plant requires a temperature of only 55–60° F. During the summer months it may be put in the open air, in the shade. It is propagated by offsets. There is a more delicate variety with leaves variegated with a yellowish-white.

CHLOROPHYTUM ELATUM

CHLOROPHYTUM elatum. Southern Africa. The numerous linear leaves, 12–16 inches long, grow in a rosette. They are light green in colour, reflexed in the upper half. More popular than the species is the variegated variety with white lines on the margins of the leaves. The small white flowers grow on a stalk much taller than the leaves. When the flowers fade, the inflorescence produces shoots which will develop into little plants. The plant prefers cool, shady situations. It is propagated easily by offsets, or by planting the plantlets from the end of the flower stalk when they have grown five or six leaves.

CORDYLINES. These plants are often called *Dracaena*, but they differ from that genus in the colour of the roots, which are white in the Cordylines and orange-yellow in the *Dracaena*. *Cordyline australis* (New Zealand) has linear lance-shaped leaves 20–24 inches long, growing in terminal clusters; these are green in the species, or variegated or striped with white or purple in the different varieties. *Cordyline stricta* (Australia) has a slender stem bearing along its entire length green linear leaves 12–16 inches long. *Cordyline bruantii* has longer leaves tinged with reddish-brown. These three species must have a temperature of 50–55° F, and can be put in the open air during the summer. *Cordyline terminalis* (Tropical Asia) differs considerably in having stalked oblong lance-shaped leaves, 12 - 20 inches long, in bronze-green; it has also produced several varieties with leaves of different reds, yellows and greens. This species requires a temperature of 65 – 70° F.

CORDYLINE TERMINALIS

DRACAENA draco (Dragon Tree). Canary Isles. In the adult state, this species has a thick, branched stem, but when it is young there is only a single stem tipped with a cluster of numerous bluey-green linear leaves, their tips extended into long points, which hang down gracefully. It is not very demanding as

DRACAENA DRACO

regards temperature (45–50° F), and is used for decorating large spaces. During the summer months it can be put in the open air.

DRACAENA sanderiana. Tropical Africa. The single slender stem carries sheathing, lance-shaped leaves 3 – 4 inches long and about 1 inch wide, which are a brilliant green with white margins. This is a more delicate species than the last, requiring a temperature of 65-70° F. The plant never reaches very large proportions, and the decorative effect is generally improved by growing three or four together in the same pot.

DRACAENA SANDERIANA

LIRIOPE graminifolia. China, Japan. A stemless plant with a short rhizome carrying narrow, linear, lance-shaped leaves 8 – 10 inches long, growing in an attractive arrangement. The small flowers are dark blue and grow on a spike 8 – 12 inches long. There is a more decorative variety with leaves variegated with whitish-blue. These are very resistant plants widely used to decorate badly lit places; they do not need a lot of heat and in winter will stand a temperature of 40 - 50° F; during the summer months they can be put in the open air. The variety with variegated leaves is rather more delicate.

LIRIOPE GRAMINIFOLIA

OPHIOPOGON JABURAN

OPHIOPOGON jaburan. Japan. An attractive plant with linear, radical leaves 12–16 inches long, reflexed at their tips. The violet-blue flowers grow in clusters that protrude only slightly from the foliage. The variety with leaves variegated with yellow is much more popular.

OPHIOPOGON japonicus (Turquoise Plant). Japan. A plant with narrow, dark green leaves from 8 – 12 inches long, and with white, lily-like flowers. It is very similar to *Liriope graminifolia*, but forms more compact clumps. The flowers produce fruits the size of a pea, which turn turquoise-blue, from which the species gets its popular name. It is very sturdy and can be planted in shady situations. Propagation is very easy, by offsets.

PHORMIUM tenax (New Zealand Flax). New Zealand. This plant, as yet not very widely grown, forms thick clumps of leaves growing from a rhizome. The leaves are upright, dark green and leathery; they may grow to a length of over 3 feet, even on a plant cultivated in a pot. The variety *variegatum*, with leaves with yellowish-white lengthwise bands, is much more sturdy and

PHORMIUM TENAX

more decorative. It requires a temperature of 45 – 50° F only during the winter and can be used to decorate verandas. In summer either a sunny or a shady place, as on a balcony, suits it well. During the winter waterings should be reduced. Propagation, which is carried out by dividing the rhizome, requires a certain background heat to encourage successful rooting.

SANSEVIERIA hahnii. This is a form which has been developed in cultivation and differs considerably from the following species. This little Sansevieria is also very sturdy. Its oblong leaves, light green with whitish-green markings, are arranged in an open rosette which gives it the appearance of some of the aloes. The varieties with leaves variegated with white or yellow are rather more delicate than the original. All the Sansevierias are propagated by division of rhizomes and by cuttings of part of the leaves. In the case of *Sansevieria hahnii*, it is better to separate the numerous offsets which as they grow tend to smother each other and become deformed. Water should be given generously during the summer months, more sparingly during the winter, especially if the plants are subjected to a drop in temperature, which should under no circumstance be allowed to fall below 54° F.

SANSEVIERIA HAHNII

SANSEVIERIA trifasciata (Sansevieria). Tropical Africa. A very familiar plant, with stiff, flat, upright leaves, 20 –

SANSEVIERIA
LAURENTII

30 inches tall, dark green with light green transverse markings. The species is now neglected in favour of the variety *laurentii*, which is generally very similar in appearance but with an attractive yellow border on the leaves. These plants stand the dry heat of some rooms very well, and do not suffer if one watering is missed or if they are left in the direct sunlight. For some tastes the leaves are too rigid, but when they are well tended they form large decorative plants, and their toleration of room conditions is certainly a point in their favour. One peculiarity is that cuttings taken from the leaves of the variety *laurentii* do not reproduce the characteristic yellow border.

VELTHEIMIA viridifolia. Southern Africa. A bulbous plant suitable for room decoration, it is interesting on account of its flowering period, which is in February, and its modest temperature requirements. The numerous oblong lance-shaped leaves, 8 – 12 inches long, are arranged in a rosette; they are a shiny dark green. The inflorescence, which grows to a height of 20 – 24 inches from the centre of the rosette, is tipped by a spike of between forty and fifty tubular pink flowers, which persist for several weeks. After the flowers have fallen, the plant continues to grow until the leaves yellow; it then enters its resting state until September-October,

VELTHEIMIA
VIRIDIFOLIA

when the bulbs will start to grow again, if left in a light place where the temperature remains at 45–50° F. Propagation is by offset bulbs and is very simple.

MARANTACEAE

CALATHEA makoyana. Brazil. This beautiful species is being seen more frequently in florists. It forms clumps of oblong leaves 12–14 inches high; the leaves are about 8 inches long and 4–6 inches wide, purple below and a shiny dark green above, with big, dark green spots on a lighter background on either side of the veins. The position of these spots gives the illusion of a compound leaf drawn on the limb of each leaf. Like the *Maranta*, this plant needs a partly shaded situation. If it is put in too much light and in too dry an atmosphere, the leaves roll up. Propagation is by offsets, but this should be left to the professional nurseryman who can provide the bottom heat necessary for this operation.

CALATHEA
MAKOYANA

MARANTA leuconeura kerchoveana. Brazil. A very pretty plant, low-growing with a procumbent stem. The leaves are oblong, heart-shaped at the base, 4 – 5 inches long and 2½ – 3 inches wide, pale green with markings on either side of the midrib which change colour as the plant grows older. Originally purplish-brown, the markings later turn a greenish-brown and finish as a dark green on old leaves. The variety *massangeana* has smaller leaves, green with a silvery sheen and with velvety-purple spots, slightly purplish below. These plants cannot stand the sun and prefer a warm, moist atmosphere in a shady situation. They need frequent watering during the summer, but less in winter, when they enter a state of partial rest.

MORACEAE

FICUS elastica (Rubber Plant). This is such a well-known, popular plant that it really needs no description. Its tolerance of room conditions and vigorous growth make it a popular choice. Under the right conditions it will grow into a very imposing plant; it requires plenty of light, a temperature between 60 – 65° F and a fairly moist atmosphere. The original species is now losing some popularity to the variety *decora*, which has rounded leaves, slightly pinkish below when young; the bract which surrounds the terminal bud before it opens is reddish, and the young

FICUS ELASTICA

leaves stay pale red for some days. There are now two varieties with variegated leaves, which deserve to be more widely grown, although they are a little more delicate than the wholly green plant.

FICUS lyrata. Tropical Africa. The leaves are leathery, longer and wider than those of the last species, and have a somewhat lyre-like shape. This plant has a more rigid appearance and is less popular than *Ficus elastica*.

FICUS pumila. China, Japan. This species has an appearance very different from *Ficus elastica*, forming low plants with trailing or climbing stems which readily attach themselves to a support by numerous adventitious roots. These slender stems carry small, oval, rounded dark green leaves 1 – 1½ inches long. *Ficus pumila* is a hardy

FICUS PUMILA

and adaptable species which can be used either as a climbing plant, trained on a frame, or grown as a hanging decoration. The variety with variegated leaves is more decorative, but grows more slowly and needs more light. It must be watered regularly and often; the soil in the pot must never be allowed to dry out or the leaves will quickly wilt and never regain their stiffness.

MUSACEAE

STRELITZIA reginae (Bird of Paradise Flower). Southern Africa. The flowers of this plant are very familiar, with their orange sepals and ultramarine petals, looking rather like the head of a bird. The flowers are often used in vases for floral decoration. The bluey-green distichous leaves, 28 – 39 inches tall, grow in a clump; from the centre of the leaves grow the inflorescences, tipped with a spathe enclosing from eight to ten flowers. Flowering is encouraged by good light and plenty of air. In winter, watering should be reduced to a bare minimum and the plants placed in a spot with a temperature of 50 – 55° F. They have numerous fleshy roots and should be potted in a heavy soil in relatively large pots. If frequent applications of liquid fertilizer are given during the growing season the plants will flower freely, and go on for three or four years without needing repotting.

STRELITZIA REGINAE

PALMACEAE

CHAMAEDOREA. Several species are popular as indoor plants. They are generally palms with a slender stem topped by a cluster of leaves which look rather thin when they are fully devel-

CHAMAEDOREA PUMILA

oped, but when young are very graceful. The most interesting of them all is *Chamaedorea pumila*, from Guatemala, which has only recently been cultivated. The stem grows to a height of 20–30 inches when fully grown, and carries about a dozen leaves, 12 – 16 inches long, consisting of lance-shaped leaflets. It tolerates room conditions well and is the only palm in which the flowers open in such conditions; although the flowers are in fact more curious than pretty. It cannot stand direct sunlight and requires frequent watering during the growing season. *Chamaedorea oblongata*, from Brazil, has a longer, slender stem, with dark green, truncated oblong leaflets; the adult plant grows well in rooms in which the temperature does not drop below 55 – 50° F during the winter.

CHAMAEROPS humilis (European Palm). Mediterranean Region. Its area of distribution once extended also to the Côte d'Azur, but today there are no representatives of the species growing there in the natural state. The stem, which does not grow over 60 inches, is topped

CHAMAEROPS HUMILIS

by a crown of leaves; it also readily gives off suckers at the base which form thick clumps. The fan-shaped leaves are divided more or less deeply into bifid segments; the leaf-stalks are long and slender, slightly compressed, with spines on either margin. Although it is not widely used today, the Dwarf Palm is a resistant, hardy plant which is very suitable for decorating a veranda or any other place where the temperature stays between 45 – 50° F. During the summer it can be put in the open air. When it is grown in a pot this plant stays smaller, never attaining a height of more than 32 inches.

HOWEA belmoreana. Lord Howe Island. Known by the name Kentia, these plants are the most widely grown of all the palms. The single stem is topped with curved leaves of linear pinnules with slightly drooping tips; in old plants the leaf-stalks are longer. To improve their decorative effect, these plants are usually grown three in a pot, forming good groups up to 5 feet high.

HOWEA BELMOREANA

PHOENIX
CANARIENSIS

HOWEA forsteriana. Lord Howe Island. This looks generally similar to the last species but is of larger dimensions when fully grown, and the leaves have small brown scales on the underside (which are not visible on young plants). The Kentias are quite strong plants, requiring an average temperature of 60 – 65° F, but they cannot stand too much light during the summer months.

PHOENIX canariensis. Canary Islands. This plant, with its rather stiff appearance, is not so popular as it was. The leaves are upright in young plants but become curved when fully grown. The dark green pinnules, tapering into extended points, are transformed at the base into long spines, which perhaps explains why the plant is becoming less popular with gardeners. It cannot tolerate high temperatures, and tends to wither in modern houses and flats, which are often overheated (another reason for its being seen less frequently nowadays). On the other hand, it is a very suitable plant for decorating halls or, during the summer, balconies – as long as they are never exposed to too much sun.

HOWEA
FORSTERIANA

PHOENIX reclinata. South-east Africa. The leaves are more upright. Also used for indoor decoration.

PHOENIX dactylifera (Date Palm). North Africa. The leaves of this palm are carried at the top of a long stem which can grow to 65 – 100 feet in warm countries. It is the palm which produces the edible fruit called the date.

RHAPIS flabelliformis. China, Japan. This stoloniferous species gives off numerous suckers which form thick clumps. The slender stems, reaching 3 – 6½ feet in height, topped by a cluster of leaves, are covered along their whole length with brown fibres. The fan-shaped leaves, deeply divided into seven to ten pendent segments, are carried on a thin stalk 8 – 10 inches long. This is the hardiest of the palms; it can stand temperatures as low as 40 – 45° F, making it highly suitable for decorating cool places. In summer, it can be put in the open air on a balcony, in a partly shaded situation. It requires frequent watering during the summer months, but little during the winter.

SYAGRUS weddelliana. Brazil. Still called *Cocos weddelliana*, this once very popular plant is now losing a little of its popularity, although its fine foliage makes it one of the most decorative species. The slender stem, covered in blackish fibres, carries numerous curved leaves, 12 - 16 inches long in young plants, with narrow pin-

SYAGRUS WEDDELLIANA

nules, coloured dark green above, silvery below. This plant is more demanding as regards warmth than *Chamaedorea pumila*, requiring a temperature of about 65° F; it must have plenty of watering and a lot of light, though it should not get the direct rays of the sun. The genus *Cocos* includes *C. nucifera* which provides the coconut; this species cannot be cultivated as an indoor plant because of its difficult growth requirements.

PINACEAE

ARAUCARIA excelsa (Norfolk Island Pine). Norfolk Island. At the beginning of the century this plant enjoyed considerable popularity, but today it is somewhat neglected in spite of its rather original appearance, like a little fir tree. The single, very straight, stem carries branches usually growing in horizontal whorls of four, forming successive tiers. The length of the branches varies with their age, but they always keep the same proportions, being larger at the base and growing shorter towards the top, giving the plant a pyramidal shape. The branches carry small needle-shaped leaves which are slightly sharp-tipped. The plant requires a temperature of only 50 – 55° F, but it must be kept in subdued light because sunlight burns the leaves.

ARAUCARIA EXCELSA

PEPEROMIA
SCANDENS

PIPERACEAE

PEPEROMIA scandens (Climbing Peperomia). Peru. Now that trailing plants are more and more popular, this species is becoming very widely used. The name suggests a climbing plant, but in fact the succulent stems, 12 – 16 inches long, either spread across the surface of the soil or hang down over the rim when grown in a pot. They carry light green leaves with rounded bases. The variegated variety is usually the only one available in this country, but it is quite widely grown as a trailing plant, and in troughs. *Peperomia scandens* is easily propagated by leaf or branch cuttings. The small flowers, growing in an upright white spike, are interesting though not very pretty.

PEPEROMIA caperata. An attractive little plant which has only recently been introduced, but has quickly won popularity. The leaves are dark green and attractively wrinkled. It is a little more delicate than the last species, and care should be taken not to wet the leaves too much when watering.

PEPEROMIA
CAPERATA

ADIANTUM CUNEATUM

POLYPODIACEAE

ADIANTUM cuneatum (Maidenhair Fern). Tropical America. This very well-known species of fern is widely used ornamentally; it forms good-sized plants 12–16 inches high, of a pretty, light green and with a very delicate appearance. This plant cannot stand dry conditions or draughts and the soil must always be kept moist. Its natural habitat is damp undergrowth, and it should not be exposed to too much full sunlight. There are numerous species of Maidenhair Fern differing only in the make-up of their fronds but otherwise looking very similar.

ASPLENIUM nidus (Bird's Nest Fern). Australia, Japan, India. This species has a very different appearance from the other ferns, with its entire fronds growing from a stout rootstock. The fronds are a brilliant green, leathery, with more or less undulate margins, and can grow to 24–28 inches long and 6 – 8 inches wide. Through the centre of the frond runs a thick black vein – an extension of the short, shiny black stalk. The arrangement of the leaves on the stock gives the whole plant the appearance of a very wide funnel. This fern cannot stand full sun,

ASPLENIUM NIDUS

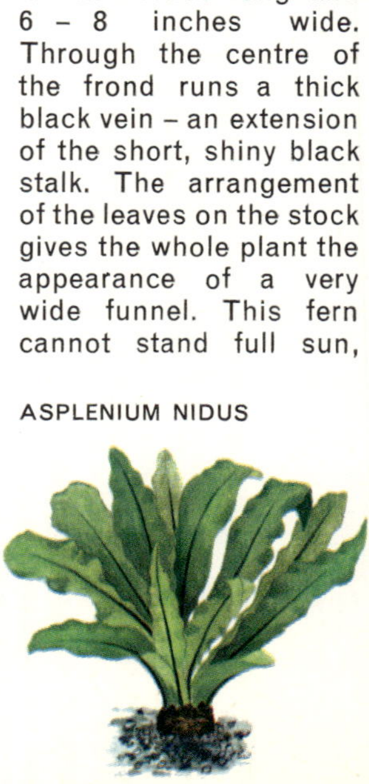

and appreciates a moist atmosphere. The rootstock is covered with hairy, interwoven roots, which look rather like a bird's nest and give the plant its name. The Bird's Nest Fern requires a winter temperature of 60° F and good light.

BLECHNUM brasiliensis (Brazilian Tree Fern). Tropical America. As it grows older, this species develops a small stipe which gives the plant an exotic appearance. The stipe forms a little trunk, up to 2 feet in height, and the fronds, which can reach a length of 30 inches, all grow from the top of it. When they first appear the fronds are pink, but they later turn green. Like all ferns, this plant requires a moist atmosphere, and cannot stand being left without water. In winter, it should be kept at a temperature of around 60° F in a well-lighted situation, but not in direct sunlight.

BLECHNUM BRASILIENSIS

BLECHNUM gibbum or **LOMARIA gibba.** New Caledonia. This is closely related to the last species, which it generally resembles, but is much more popular. It is smaller in all ways and is more suitable for room decoration.

NEPHROLEPIS exaltata. Tropical regions. A fern with numerous

NEPHROLEPIS EXALTATA

fronds which form thick clumps 2 – 3 feet tall. If it is kept away from direct sunlight, in a moist atmosphere, it is hardy enough to grow happily indoors in an average temperature of 60° F, but it cannot stand being left dry. Plants of this genus are interesting because they readily produce stolons, which give rise to little plants which can be used to propagate them.

NEPHROLEPIS cordifolia. Tropical regions. Compared with the last species, the fronds of this plant are simpler and less dense; the plant itself is hardier and can stand lower temperatures.
Nephrolepis species are particularly useful for planting in hanging baskets in greenhouses and conservatories. The baskets are usually lined with moss and half filled, with a compost of loam and leafmould and topped up with soil, the plants are then set in this mixture, where they soon establish themselves. They can be hung outside during the summer, but the soil must never be allowed to become dry or the plants become yellow and wither.

PELLAEA rotundifolia. New Zealand. This small fern forms very rounded clumps. The fronds, 8 –

NEPHROLEPIS CORDIFOLIA

10 inches tall, give off blackish-brown, scaly, downy stalks. These carry, here and there, dark green, roundish pinnules, numbering between ten and twenty, depending on the strength of the plant.

PELLAEA hastata. Southern Africa. This species differs from the last in having larger bipinnate fronds, 12 – 16 inches long, and larger, slightly hastate pinnules. The stalk, which is a little hairy at the base, and the rachis are both reddish.

PELLAEA HASTATA

The *Pellaea rotundifolia* grows well in a temperature of 50 - 55° F, the *Pellaea hastata* needs more warmth. Both of them should be put in shady situations; they require slightly less humidity than the other ferns.

PLATYCERIUM alcicorne (Stag's Horn Fern). Australia. This fern, only quite recently added to the range of indoor plants, is one of the most curious and at the same time one of the most decorative of the true ferns. The sterile fronds are entire, rounded, and grow in tight clusters, one on top of the other. The fertile fronds, growing upright or at a slight angle, are 12 - 20 inches long, downy, and divided at the tip into two segments, each of which is further divided into two, giving the frond an antler-like appearance. This plant readily gives off adventitious buds, so that it will form large clumps, especially if it is grown

in a ball of moss on a wooden support; the buds grow through the moss and as they develop, completely cover the support. It should be grown in a spot shaded from direct sunlight; it will not be seriously harmed if the watering is forgotten occasionally.

POLYPODIUM aureum. Tropical America. This beautiful and hardy plant really deserves to be more widely used in indoor decoration. It is a fern with large fronds, reaching over 3 feet in height, with a stalk and rachis the colour of mahogany. The fronds are deeply cut into ten to twelve segments, forming linear, lance-shaped pinnules with a slight bluey-green bloom on both surfaces. The decorative effect of the plant is heightened by the rust-coloured sori, which grow about $\frac{1}{8}$ inch apart in a line along the midrib of the pinnules. The fronds arise from a thick rhizome, completely covered in golden scales, growing on the surface of the soil. This species is semi-epiphytic, and requires a compost containing a high proportion of organic matter. It prefers a shady situation, and is not harmed by an occasional lack of water. Propagation presents no difficulties; short lengths can be cut off the rhi-

zome and treated as adult plants. In winter the temperature should be kept at about 60° F.

POLYSTICHUM falcatum. Polynesia, New Zealand. This fern has leathery fronds growing out of the centre of the plant, from the top of a short stem; the rachis is 16–20 inches long, slightly reflexed, and covered along its whole length with brown scales. The pinnules, arranged on

POLYSTICHUM FALCATUM

either side of the rachis, are a brilliant green, and sickle shaped with a slightly rounded base. The variety *rochefordii* has larger pinnules with a coarsely toothed margin. This very hardy fern, as yet not widely cultivated, grows well in indoor conditions; it is quite happy in a fairly low temperature (55–60° F). During the summer months it can be put in the open air in a shaded situation. Like all ferns it needs a fairly high humidity.

PTERIS cretica. Tropical and subtropical regions. Along with the maidenhairs this is one of the most popular ferns, but it is not as delicate as the maidenhairs. The fronds are 16 – 20 inches tall, with blackish stalks and finely toothed, green linear pinnules 4 – 5 inches long and about ½ inch wide, the lower two of which are bifid. This species has given rise to several varieties, of which the most interesting are:

albo lineata, a spreading plant with rather fewer pinnules, coloured dark green with a white central band, the terminal

PTERIS CRETICA

ones being considerably longer and the basal ones bifid;

wimsetii, generally similar to the original species, with polymorphic, simple or branched fronds much divided at their tips.

PTERIS ensiformis. Tropical Asia. A species with fronds 8 – 10 inches long; the pinnules are narrower than in the last species, divided, and coloured a lighter green, with a more or less regular whitish line which runs along the midrib, sometimes spreading to cover the whole surface of the pinnule.

All the pteris suffer from too much direct sunlight and lack of moisture; they appreciate a moist atmosphere and a temperature of 55 – 60° F.

PUNICACEAE

PUNICA granatum (Pomegranate). Southern Europe. This species is a shrub which is cultivated in some areas for its fruit, the pomegranate. It reaches a height of 9 – 12 feet or more, but there is a dwarf form known as *Punica granata nanum* which grows only to about 18 inches in height and forms an attractive little shrub. It is a regular, much branched plant with light green leaves and numerous brilliant red flowers, which are later replaced by tiny pomegranates. It is not very demanding;

PUNICA GRANATUM

in the summer it likes good light and ample fresh air, and can be grown on a balcony. At the end of October the leaves yellow and fall; the plant should then be put in a cool place and the waterings reduced. At the end of April, when growth starts again, it should be put once more in the open air. The variety *nana racemosa* has double flowers.

CITRUS SINENSIS

RUTACEAE

CITRUS sinensis (Orange Tree). Asia. A fruit tree intensively cultivated for the production of oranges. When it is grown in a pot, the orange tree forms attractive bushes which keep their dark green leaves throughout the year. They are very hardy if they are kept in winter at a temperature of 40 – 45° F, and during the summer get plenty of air. Older plants flower regularly; the fragrant white flowers give rise to small oranges which are very decorative but cannot be eaten. These plants can be propagated easily by planting the seeds from the oranges.

CITRUS japonica (Kumquat). Japan. Compared with *Citrus sinensis*, this species forms more compact and more attractive bushes when grown in a pot. It also has the advantage that its flowers, which are also fragrant and white in colour, produce small orange-coloured fruits which are edible, including their peel.

SAXIFRAGACEAE

SAXIFRAGA sarmentosa (Roving Sailor). China, Japan. This plant grows in a rosette formed by numerous long-stalked leaves, 4 – 6 inches long. The leaves are rounded, crenate, mat green with white veins above and reddish below. The inflorescence consists of a panicle, 10 – 12 inches tall, with white flowers.

SAXIFRAGA fortunei. Japan. The leaves of this species are smaller than in *Saxifraga sarmentosa*, green, and dentate. The variety *tricolor* is very decorative, with leaves variegated with pink, yellow and white, but is a little more delicate and needs a situation with good light, shaded from the direct rays of the sun. These three saxifrages produce runners in the same way as the strawberry and are good as hanging plants. In winter they should be watered only lightly to avoid rotting. The runners can be easily separated from the parent to propagate new plants.

SAXIFRAGA SARMENTOSA

TOLMIEA menziesii (Pick-a-Back Plant). North America. Although it is not very widely grown in England, this is an interesting plant which grows to a good size; the leaves are rounded, covered with silky hairs, which are found also on the 4 – 6 inch leaf-stalks. The inflorescences, which are similar to those of the saxifrages, rarely appear on cultivated plants, and when they do

TOLMIEA MENZIESII

the flowers produce no seed: they are self-sterile. The plant has the strange feature of producing young plants on the older leaves. New plants can be propagated by simply detaching them from the parent and planting them in the soil. *Tolmiea menziesii* likes a lot of light and plenty of water during the summer months. In winter, the plant should be put in a cool spot and kept on the dry side until the following spring.

SELAGINELLACEAE

SELAGINELLA martensii (Selaginella). Mexico. This plant, which is very popular in florists' shops, is commonly thought to be a fern. It does, in fact, have similar requirements as regards temperature and situation and in the attention it needs. It forms low clumps 8 – 12 inches high, the numerous stems spreading at first, then growing upwards and branching at the tip. They are covered along their entire length with small green scale-like leaves. The variety *watsoniana* is more decora-

SELAGINELLA MARTENSII

tive, with silvery-white tips to the branches. Like the ferns these plants do not produce flowers. They are easily propagated from cuttings; the stems readily give off adventitious roots. It is important never to let the soil in the pot dry out.

SOLANACEAE

SOLANUM capsicastrum (Winter Cherry). Madeira. This little shrub makes a very attractive pot-plant. It is branched, with pale-green, oblong, lance-shaped leaves. The flowers are small and white, and are of no great decorative value. They do, however, produce round fruits about the size of a small cherry, which ripen to a bright scarlet colour and persist on the plant throughout the autumn and for part of the winter. The plants do not require a high temperature and can be grown perfectly well at 50–55° F. During the summer months they can be stood outdoors, where the fruits set more freely. The fruits set numerous seeds, which can be sown to produce young plants the following year.

SOLANUM CAPSICASTRUM

THEACEAE

CAMELLIA japonica. Japan. Camellias were very widely grown at the beginning of this century, both for their flowers, used as cut flowers, and as a pot-plant. It is an evergreen shrub with shiny, dark-green leaves, which has the great advantage that it flowers in February-March. Depending on the variety, the flowers may be single or double, white, pink, red or variegated. During the summer, the plants should be put in the open air in a shaded situation. They should be watered frequently during the time when the flower buds are developing. At the end of October the plants should be taken under cover, in a cool greenhouse where there is plenty of light, and given as much fresh air as possible. During the winter, the temperature can drop to 40° F without harming them. In this cool, fresh atmosphere the flowers will open in early spring, provided they are grown in a lime-free compost.

CLEYERA FORTUNEI

CAMELLIA JAPONICA

CLEYERA fortunei. China, Japan. This plant is often incorrectly called *Eurya japonica*, and is in fact not widely known by its real name. It is a small bush, which may grow to over 30 inches, with persistent oblong, lance-shaped leaves, 2–3 inches long, of a brilliant green variegated with yellow. In the young plant these leaves are pink.

Cleyera fortunei can be used to decorate places where the temperature during the winter is between 45–50°F. During the summer months it should be put in the open, in a situation with plenty of light. The small white flowers are not very decorative. Like the *Camellia*, these plants should be potted in lime-free loam, leaf-mould and peat and if possible given only rain water.

TILIACEAE

SPARMANNIA africana (African Hemp). Southern Africa. This plant sometimes reaches a height of over 3 feet. It is branched, with lobed, heartshaped leaves covered on both surfaces and on their stalks with silky hairs. The flowers have large stamens, yellow at the base and red at the tips, contrasting with the white petals, which grow in umbels at the ends of the branches. The plant flowers in spring, or sometimes earlier if kept under favourable conditions (a temperature of 45–50° F during the winter). In a dry atmosphere the leaves soon fall off. During the summer months, the plants can be stood outdoors, provided they are given plenty of water.

URTICACEAE

PILEA cadierei (Aluminium Plant). Indochina. This plant was introduced into Europe in 1938

SPARMANNIA
AFRICANA

PILEA
CADIEREI

and became very popular; it is now widely grown throughout the whole world. It forms clumps 10 – 12 inches tall, with leaves 3 – 4 inches long, coloured green with white markings along either side of the midrib and on the margins. These plants can stand shaded situations, but they will only grow there slowly; to obtain a large size, they need situations with plenty of light. They are propagated easily by cuttings from young shoots, which should be inserted three per pot in 3-inch pots to obtain sizeable plants more quickly.

VITACEAE

CISSUS antarctica (Kangaroo Vine). Australia. This species, recently introduced as an indoor plant, is particularly valuable because it can grow perfectly well in shady situations. It can be trained on a frame, or grown as a trailing or hanging plant. The flexible branches carry simple, oval leaves with slightly toothed margins, coloured a brilliant green on the upper surface; they also have tendrils by which they cling to their supports. The plant is

CISSUS
ANTARCTICA

RHOICISSUS RHOMBOIDEA

easily propagated by layering or by cuttings. It is a fairly hardy plant and will thrive at a temperature of 45 – 50° F.

CISSUS striata. Chile. A species with reddish twining stems carrying numerous leaves; these are compound, with five dark green leaflets toothed only at their tips. It is more tender than *Cissus antarctica* and appears to require more water.

RHOICISSUS rhomboidea. Southern Africa. This climbing plant is one of the most good-natured and has the advantage that it will thrive even in dim light. The leaves are compound, each with three leaflets, green with light brown veins. The stem carries a single tendril. The plant cannot stand direct sunlight or a dry atmosphere; to get a well-developed specimen, the situation must be chosen carefully. The branches can be trained on a frame or trellis. The temperature should be 55 – 60° F. Propagation is by cuttings of branches.

CISSUS STRIATA

SUCCULENT PLANTS

AIZOACEAE

FENESTRARIA rhopalophylla (Windowed Plant). Southern Africa. This plant, really more of a curiosity than a decoration, is now included in the mesembryanthemums (ice plants). It consists of a rosette of light green conical leaves, 2 – 2½ inches long, with the base of the cone forming the tip of the leaf; at the tip there is a transparent area called a 'window'. This window has no function in plants grown in the home, but in the wild it is vital. To survive the dry season the plant buries itself almost entirely in the ground, exposing only its windows, through which it gets the sunlight it needs for photosynthesis. The long-stalked white flowers, 1 – 1½ inches across, appear in October.

FENESTRARIA RHOPALOPHYLLA

AMARYLLIDACEAE

A G A V E americana (American Aloe or Sisal Plant). Mexico. This species has become acclimatized in various regions of Southern Europe particularly the South of France, where plants grow to full size and flower outdoors. When grown in a pot, the plant stays much smaller. The leaves grow in a rosette; they are thick, leathery, glaucous, slightly inflexed in the upper part, and have a border of hooked spines and a long black spine at the tip.

The variety *marginata* has leaves variegated with yellow; it is just as hardy as the original species. The American Aloe flowers only when it has attained its full size, so that the inflorescence never opens in plants grown indoors. But this has the advantage that it extends the life of the plant, which normally dies after flowering. The Aloe needs the sun and plenty of air. In winter, it likes a low temperature (about 40–45° F). It is propagated by simply detaching the offshoots which the plant readily produces.

AGAVE victoriae reginae. Mexico. A beautiful species, which looks rather different from the other plants in the same genus. The leaves are numerous, triangular in cross-section, dark green with whitish lines, and attain a height of 8 – 10

AGAVE
VICTORIAE REGINAE

inches in the fully grown plant. They form a spherical rosette. Each leaf is tipped with a stiff black spine. This is a very hardy plant which can be put out of doors during the summer months. In winter, waterings should be less frequent. This species does not produce offshoots and reproduces only by seeds; for this reason it is comparatively rare.

AGAVE ferdinandi regis. This is very similar to the last species, differing only in having two or three small spines at the tip. Both these plants are very small and can be kept for a long time as a decoration in the home.

ASCLEPIADACEAE

CARALLUMA buchardii. Canary Islands. This plant has grey-green stems, quadrangular in cross-section and 4 – 10 inches tall, which give off branches at the base to form quite big clumps. The leaves are tiny, only a fraction of an inch long; they grow from the angles of the stem and are very short-lived. The flowers are stalkless and just over ½ inch across, coloured brown with numerous white hairs, and grow in clusters in the upper part of the stem.

AGAVE FERDINANDI

CARALLUMA BUCHARDII

CARALLUMA DECAISNEANA

CARALLUMA decaisneana. Senegal. This species has almost cylindrical stems, with four very blunt angles carrying small soft spines. The stems are light green with reddish-brown marbling, and have a shiny appearance. The flowers are dark brown and larger than those of the last species.

These plants must be put in sunlight. During the winter, watering should be reduced, for too much water will definitely cause the stems to rot. Both species need a lot of light and a temperature of 47 – 50° F.

CEROPEGIA fusca. Canary Islands. This plant, consisting of cylindrical stems, is really more of a curiosity than a decoration. The stems are very stiff, greeny-brown when young, but becoming whitish with age; young shoots, at the time that they appear, carry narrow leaves 1½ inches long. The flowers are tubular, brown outside and yellow inside, and grow clustered round the stem at the nodes.

CEROPEGIA DICHOTOMA

CEROPEGIA FUSCA

CEROPEGIA dichotoma. Canary Islands. This is closely related to the last species, but has taller, branched, pale green stems and yellowish-brown flowers.

Both these species can pass the winter in a spot where the temperature is constant at between 47 – 50° F. During this period hardly any water should be given. The plant is propagated easily by cuttings taken from the stem.

CEROPEGIA woodii (Hearts Entwined). Natal. Although it belongs to the same genus as the last species, this plant is very different in appearance and growth. The bulb produces slender, trailing stems that may reach a length of 5 feet. The leaves are opposite, heart-shaped, rounded and fleshy, coloured green variegated with greenish-white. The flowers are tubular, pale violet, and have fringed lobes which curve back and are united by their tips above the tube.

CEROPEGIA debilis. Tropical Africa. This is generally very similar to the last species, but has elongated leaves.

In both these species, the small bulbs which form

on the stem at the nodes can be used for propagation. Both should be grown as hanging plants, at a temperature of about 60° F and in a situation with plenty of light.

HUERNIA penzigii. Ethiopia. This plant forms compact clumps of branches, none of which grow to more than about 4 inches in length. The branches are green, five-

HUERNIA PENZIGII

sided, and carry on the angles soft spines about half an inch long; they never produce leaves. The flowers are purplish-black and open wide, measuring up to 1 inch across. Unlike those of the *Caralluma*, they appear at the bases of the branches.

HUERNIA PILLAN

HUERNIA pillansii. Cape Province. This plant has almost-globular stems, their numerous ribs are covered with soft spines about ⅛ inch long, and are usually recurved. The flowers form a five-pointed star with their widespread triangular lobes, which are pale green and covered with crimson papillae. These plants are very susceptible to rotting,

STAPELIA VARIEGATA

and during the winter should be given very little water and plenty of light.

STAPELIA variegata (Carrion Flower). Southern Africa. This plant is identical to *Calluma* and *Huernia* except that the stems, quadrangular in section and about 4 inches tall, carry on the angles teeth which gradually lengthen into points. In young plants, these teeth have very small green laminae which function as leaves, but these very soon fall off. The branches are green, but often take on a purple colour when the plants are exposed to strong sunlight. The single flowers are 2½ – 3 inches wide, with triangular, pale-green lobes spotted with purple marbling. They grow on a stalk 1½ – 2 inches long. This plant has the same requirements as those of the last two genera described. It is propagated by cuttings from a branch but these should be planted out at a sharp angle as the roots develop on the side and not on the cut end as in other plants. The flowers give off a disagreeable odour, which attracts flies to pollinate them.

STAPELIA grandiflora. Southern Africa. The stems of this plant are distinctly four-sided,

STAPELIA GRANDIFLORA

green, downy, and can grow to a height of 1 foot. The flowers are very large, 5 – 6 inches across, with triangular, lance-shaped, dark brown lobes covered with purplish hairs; they are carried on a short stalk about ½ inch long growing from the base of the stems.

STAPELIA gigantea. Transvaal. This species has a huge flower which can grow to 28 inches in diameter; the lobes are acuminate, yellow with irregular purple transverse lines, and covered all over with long, spreading, silky hairs.
Unfortunately, the flowers of both these species give off a rather unpleasant odour. They require very little water during the winter.

DYCKIA ALTISSIMA

BROMELIACEAE

DYCKIA altissima. Brazil. The plants of this genus belong to the same family as the epiphytic *Tillandsia*, but because of their adaptation to a dry climate they are grouped among the thick-leaved plants. The leaves are thick and leathery, bordered with spines, green above and whitish below, and grow in a rosette. The orange-red flowers grow in a spike at the tip of an inflorescence 24 – 32 inches tall. These plants are very tolerant of room conditions; they need a sunny situation and should be watered

STAPELIA GIGANTEA

only lightly in the winter. They do not suffer if left without water, even for some length of time.

There are also other species which can be used for indoor decoration: *Dyckia brevifolia*, which has shorter leaves, and *Dyckia rariflora*, in which the leaves are grooved on the upper surface. All three species are cultivated for their leaves.

FASCICULARIA pitcairniifolia. Chile. A stemless plant consisting of numerous leaves growing in a rosette. The leaves are 10 – 16 inches long and just under 1 inch wide, leathery and bordered with spines, and strongly reflexed in the upper half. The small violet flowers appear at the centre of the rosette and are short-lived. At the time of flowering, the bases of the central leaves take on a beautiful red colour that contrasts strongly with the dark green of the leaves; the plant keeps this colouring for several months. It is very tough and needs strong sunlight, and during the winter can be kept at a temperature of about 50° F. After flowering, the rosette dies, but by this time it has given off several shoots which can be detached and replanted to propagate the plant.

FASCICULARIA PITCAIRNIIFOLIA

CACTACEAE

APOROCACTUS flagelliformis. Mexico. This very common species, the most widely grown, is one of the most attractive in spring, when the flowers appear; these may be very abundant. The stems are slender and much branched at the base; they are just over ½ inch in diameter but can grow to a length of over 3 feet. At first they are upright, but soon start to hang down. The stems have ten or twelve ribs, carrying from ten to twelve reddish-brown radiating needles and three or four central needles, brown at the base and yellow at the tip. The flowers are purplish-red, 3–4 inches long, with the petals arranged in a series of whorls, one partly overlapping the other. They stay open for three or four days. This plant likes a situation with plenty of sun, and frequent watering in the summer; in winter, waterings should be reduced, to allow the plant to enter a state of partial rest. If these three conditions are observed, it should be possible to obtain a large number of flowers. It is a species which is very suitable for use as a hanging plant.

APOROCACTUS FLAGELLIFORMIS

ASTROPHYTUM asterias. Mexico. This plant always represents the centre-piece of any collection, the pride and joy of its owner. It is always wider than it is tall, a good example measuring about 2 inches by 3 inches or more. The ribs are very flat and are separated by narrow, shallow grooves; each rib has a line of areoles down the centre, in the form of little whitish woolly cush-

ASTROPHYTUM ASTERIAS

ions which have no needles. This arrangement of lines of areoles and geometric grooves, on a background of green speckled with white dots, is peculiar to the plants of this genus and produces a very attractive effect even before the flowers appear. The flowers are yellow with a red centre, about 2 inches across, and grow at the centre of the plant. This is a rather delicate species which should be watered only lightly in summer and kept completely dry during the winter. Grafted plants have a stronger constitution.

ASTROPHYTUM myriostigma (Bishop's Mitre). Mexico. This species gets its usual name from the arrangement of its five regular and deeply divided ribs, which look rather like a cardinal's cap. It is a plant which deserves a place in every collection. It has a very characteristic appearance: the epidermis is green but looks white because it is densely covered with a huge number of small white dots; each of these dots is really a minute

ASTROPHYTUM MYRIOSTIGMA

tuft of tiny white hairs which can be seen quite clearly under even a small magnifying-glass. This is one of the cacti which has no spines. It can attain a height of 20 inches, but usually it grows no larger than an orange. Several flowers, about 3 inches across, appear in succession at the centre of the plant. There are other forms of this plant with four, six or eight ribs.

ASTROPHYTUM ornatum. Mexico. Unlike the last species, all of the eight ribs of this cactus have areoles with five or six radiating spines up to 1½ inches long and a longer, stronger central spine, all of which are yellow at first, becoming brownish later. The epidermis is covered with small woolly tufts, larger and more widely spaced than in *Astrophytum myriostigma*. In its native habitat, this plant grows into a column which can attain a height of over 3 feet and a diameter of 1 foot. When cultivated in our climate it stays much smaller, a height of 8 – 12 inches achieved in a very good specimen. The flower is light yellow and measures about 3 inches across. In all the species in this genus, it is found that the size of the flower is in proportion to the size of the plant.

ASTROPHYTUM ORNATUM

CEPHALOCEREUS palmeri or **PILOSOCEREUS palmeri.** Mexico. The stem of this plant is in the form of a branched column, blue-green or glaucous, with about eight wide, rounded and

CEPHALOCEREUS PALMERI

well-defined ribs; it can reach a height of 13 feet. The areoles are very woolly, with greyish-white hairs 1-1½ inches long, which are often tangled; longer, denser hairs which appear on one side of the stem near the top of the plant indicate where and when the flowers will develop. Growing among the woolly hairs on each areole are eight to twelve spreading spines about half an inch long, and one or two central spines; these are yellow, stronger and longer than the others, growing to a length of over 1 inch. The flowers, which open at night, are about 3 inches long, pink or pale pink on the inside and a reddish-green outside. This cactus is easy to grow and is often seen in collections. It can stand poor light, but it must have a warm, moist atmosphere. It can be propagated very easily by cuttings. In our climate, the flower rarely appears and the plant grows to only quite a small size.

CEPHALOCEREUS senilis (Old Man Cactus). Mexico. The long white hairs, which can grow to a length of a few inches, depending on the size of the plant, have earned this species its common name. All that can be seen of the plant is the thick bush of hairs, hiding the epidermis which consists of about thirty small sinuous ribs. The long hairs are formed by highly modified spines spreading from the areoles, numbering about thirty on each; among them also appear two to five yellow spines grow-

CEPHALOCEREUS SENILIS

ing to no more than 2 inches in length. This species does not flower in our climate. It is a slow-growing plant which likes a warm, sunny situation and needs frequent watering in summer, but must be given no water at all in winter. Care should be taken not to get water on the hairs.

CEREUS peruvianus. Brazil, Mexico. This plant was first described in 1623 and was the first species of columnar cactus to be imported into Europe. In spite of its name, it does not originate from Peru. In its native habitat, this species can grow to a height of about 50 feet, with numerous lateral branches; the young plant appears as an upright stem with five to eight ribs. The areoles each give rise to about seven spines up to ½ inch long, and a stron-

CEREUS PERUVIANUS

ger central spine; these spines all lengthen as the plant grows and can reach a length of over 2 inches. The flowers appear only on older plants; they are tubular, 4 – 6 inches long and about 5 inches wide, with petals white on the inside and pink or brown outside, and greenish-red sepals; they open only at night. The variety *monstruosus*, commonly known as the Living Rock, has twisted ribs and forms a mass of small irregular branches. This variety does not flower but its unusual shape makes it quite decorative. The species is very resistant to indoor conditions.

CHAMAECEREUS silvestrii. Argentina. This little cactus forms compact groups of shoots, these break off easily and can be used as cuttings. The numerous stems branch readily, and grow up to 4 inches in length and ½ inch thick. They have from eight to ten sides meeting at rather blunt angles, and the densely set areoles each produce ten to fifteen tiny white spreading spines and one slightly longer central spine. The wide, funnel-shaped, glowing, red flowers are very large in relation to the size of the plant: 2½ inches long and 2–2½ inches in diameter. The plant is very hardy and requires good light, frequent watering in summer and plenty of air. In winter the soil should be kept very slightly moist and the plant placed in a cool situation. The abundant flowers appear in May. The plant can be propagated very easily by cuttings and there are a number of well-known hybrids of this species.

CHAMAECEREUS SILVESTRII

CLEISTOCACTUS strausii. Bolivia. The stem of this cactus grows erect to a height of about 5 feet, with a diameter of about 3 inches; it gives off no branches but sends out numerous shoots at the base. The stems are light green and have twenty five ribs with areoles growing quite close together. Each areole has three or four light-yellow, central spines growing downwards through a mass of thirty to forty long (over ½ inch) white hairs, which represent the spreading spines. This species is particularly attractive when it grows to a good size and develops several stems. The tubular red flowers, about 3 inches long, grow horizontally from the stem near the top.

ECHINOCEREUS blanckii. Mexico. This plantis upright at first, but with age tends to grow along the ground. The dark-green branches can reach a length of 12 to 14 inches and a diameter of over 1 inch. The five or six ribs are covered with tubercles, on the tips of which are the areoles; these have eight or nine spreading spines about ½ inch long, some shining black, others white or whitish and black, and one to three central spines up to 1 inch long. The flowers are somewhat elongated, about 4 inches long, with wide violet petals; they usually appear in great abundance, making the plant a very handsome sight. The plant is propagated

ECHINOCEREUS BLANCKII

easily by cuttings taken from the numerous branches. It is very hardy, and can stand temperatures below freezing and in some places can be grown in beds in the open. It does require a situation with very good light.

ECHINOCEREUS engelmannii. California, Mexico. This cactus is mostly known for its very decorative spines. The branches, 6 – 8 inches long and about 2 inches in diameter, often grow upright and have eleven to fourteen blunt ribs. The light-green colour of the epidermis is hardly visible under the thick covering of spines, ten to twelve spreading spines to each areole, ½ inch long, and four to six spines growing centrally, more or less twisted, to 3 inches long. The spines range in colour from yellowish to red-brown. Sometimes variegated spines may be seen on a plant. The flower, with its purple-red petals, is 2 to 3 inches across and almost as long. This is a slow-growing species.

ECHINOPSIS aurea or LOBIVIA aurea. Argentina. This is a little globular cactus which sometimes becomes cylindrical with age and gives off few buds or none at all. The stem is light green, with about fifteen sharp-angled ribs. The four central spines are 1

ECHINOPSIS AUREA

inch long and slightly flattened; the eight spreading spines, which are a little shorter, are off-white. The attractive lemon-yellow flowers, carried on a slender tube covered with small greyish hairs, grow to about 3½ inches long and 3 inches in diameter. The plant is easily propagated by seeds. It is popular with collectors because of its flowers, and because it is easy to grow and takes up little room. It is rather like a miniature *Echinopsis eyriesii*, but is distinguished by the tube of the flower, which is much shorter, and by the colour, which is never yellow in *Echinopsis eyriesii*.

ECHINOPSIS eyriesii. Uruguay. This is one of the best-known cacti, and is probably the most widely grown because it is so easily propagated by cuttings from its shoots. It is globular at first, later becoming columnar and reaching a height, in cultivation, of 20 - 24 inches and a diameter of about 6 inches. It has about ten deeply divided ribs, often more. Projecting from the whitish wool of the areoles are about fourteen black spines, very short (at most $^1/_5$ inch), cylindrical and thick at the base. The flowers, white with a green pistil, are very pretty and fragrant; they are trumpet-shaped, 8 –

ECHINOPSIS EYRIESII

10 inches long and 4 – 5 inches wide at the tip, and the tube is covered with scales and long, fine, brown hairs; they appear on the plant in June-July and open out at dusk; by the early

ECHINOPSIS MULTIPLEX

morning they have wilted. Plants which give off a lot of shoots flower less.

ECHINOPSIS multiplex. Southern Brazil. This species gives off abundant vegetative buds, which make propagation very simple. It is often confused with *Echinopsis eyriesii*, which it resembles in general appearance, having more or less the same number of ribs. But it differs in its spines: the spreading spines, eight to fifteen on each areole, yellowish-brown with darker tips, becoming whitish later, are ½ – ¾ inch long, and the brown central spines, one to three in number, grow to 1 – 1½ inches. The flowers are the same size as on *Echinopsis eyriesii* but pink; they are trumpet-shaped and grow from the side of the stem near the top, on old areoles. Fully grown plants flower profusely. The flower opens for several days and gives off a rather strong scent of jasmine or vanilla.

ESPOSTOA lanata. Ecuador, Peru. This upright columnar cactus is often seen in collections. It is characterized by its abundant woolly growth, which is thicker in the

ESPOSTOA LANATA

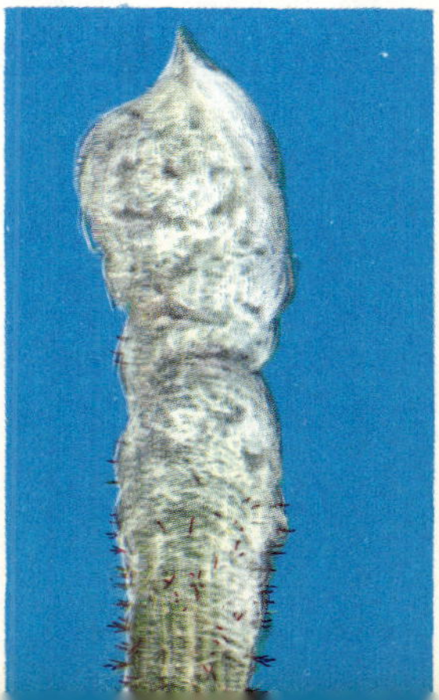

upper part of the plant. The stem is light green and has about twenty ribs carrying numerous areoles. These produce the woolly covering and also about fifteen reddish spreading spines, of which one or two growing in the centre of the areole are longer, up to 3 inches, yellowish at the base and red at the tip. This species grows slowly. It does perfectly well on its own roots, but is often found grafted on *Cereus spachianus*. It requires quite a lot of warmth, but will do equally well in full sunlight or in a partly shaded situation. The pinkish-white flower does not appear under our climatic conditions, but, after all, this species is not grown for its bloom. The variety *sericata* has lateral spines about ¼ inch long, light-coloured like the central spine. The flowers are whitish inside, and pink on the outside. The covering of woolly hairs is denser and coloured white with a yellow tinge.

EPIPHYLLUM BRIDGESII

EPIPHYLLUM bridgesii or **SCHLUMBERGERA bridgesii.** Christmas Cactus or Crab Cactus. Brazil. In its native habitat, this plant lives not on the soil but on the trees of virgin forests, where it finds nourishment in accumulations of vegetable debris, like the related Orchids. It is characterized by having many segments, flattened like leaves, growing end on end and branching often. The flowers are very beautiful and grow at the tips of these segments, reaching a length of about 3 inches.

They are asymmetrical, with petals growing in several layers. They are diurnal, odourless, pink to red in colour. The plant makes a splendid sight when all its flowers appear, almost at once, around Christmas time. It should be grown in humus-bearing soil, and during the summer should be put in the open air, in the shade.

FEROCACTUS echidne. Central Mexico. The genus *Ferocactus* is characterized by a rather massive general appearance and a heavy covering of strong spines. *Ferocactus echidne* is globular, in our climate producing few, if any, suckers, although in its native habitat it can have about twenty heads and so attain a very large size. The stem is light green, with thirteen or fourteen strong, slightly undulate ribs. The areoles are elongate, about 1 inch apart, with seven to nine spines, irregular and slightly curved, up to 1 inch long, and a strong, straight central spine about 1½ inches long, growing perpendicularly or at a slight angle. The flowers are about 1 inch long, with brilliant yellow inside and greenish-yellow outside petals.

FEROCACTUS ECHIDNE

FEROCACTUS latispinus. Mexico. This plant has a greyish-green body, globular, flattened on top, which can grow to a height of 12 inches and a diameter of 15 – 16 inches. Depending on age, it has from eight to twenty ribs with areoles set in depressions, from which arise ten to twelve wide-spreading slender spines, annulated, white or reddish, up to 1 inch long, and four stronger central spines, also annulated, red — becoming lighter with age. The three upper central spines are spreading, stiff, slightly flattened, and the lower central spine, which is larger than the others, is annulated, flat, downward pointing, hooked at the tip, and about 1¼ inches long and ¼ inch wide. The flower is central, 1 – 1½ inches long; the colour varies with the individual — from pink to purple.

FEROCACTUS LATISPINUS

GYMNOCALYCIUM BALDIANUM

GYMNOCALYCIUM baldianum. Argentina. The body of this plant is bluish green, globular, flattened at the top, and about 2 inches across, with nine to twelve wide, rounded ribs covered with tubercles. Above the tubercles are the areoles, from which arise five wide-spreading greyish spines about ½ inch long, two on each side and one pointing downwards; there is no central spine. The flower is nearly 2 inches long and grows from the top of the plant; the outer petals are greenish red, the inner ones are a magnificent blood-red — the deepest shade of red of all the plants of this genus. All these species flower readily and have the advantage that they open their corollas for several days. Multiplication of *Gymnocalycium baldianum* is by seeds only, as it does not give off side shoots.

GYMNOCALYCIUM denudatum. Argentina, Brazil, Paraguay, Uruguay. This attractive plant is not very common and is quite popular with collectors. As its botanical name suggests, this plant has only a very poor covering of spines. The broadly globular body, wider than it is tall, is a shining dark green; it can grow to about 4 inches in height and 6 inches across. It has five to eight wide, blunt ribs, separated by narrow grooves. The rounded areoles carry five to eight yellowish-white lateral spines about ½ inch long; these spread sinuously across the plant body, looking rather like the legs of a

GYMNOCALYCIUM DENUDATUM

spider. The flower is 2 – 3 inches long, with green, white-bordered outer petals which are reflexed when the flower is fully open, white central petals and pinkish-white intermediate petals.

GYMNOCALYCIUM lafaldense or GYMNOCALYCIUM bruchii. Argentina. This is the smallest plant of the genus *Gymnocalycium*, measuring only about 1 inch across and 1½ – 2 inches in height. It consists of twelve ribs divided into closely packed tubercles. The areoles carry twelve to fifteen

GYMNOCALYCIUM BRUCHII

small, bristly, white, spreading spines about $^{1}/_{5}$ inch long, which form a delicate covering, and sometimes a single dark-coloured central spine. This little plant branches freely and forms dense clumps; at the same time, a large number of shoots are given off at the base. The flowers, just over 1 inch long and about as wide, coloured a delicate light violet, completely cover the plant. This species is grown for its attractive, often abundant flowers; it also has the advantage that flowers appear on young plants which are still less than ½ inch across.

HAMATOCACTUS setispinus. Southern Texas and northern Mexico. The appeal of this plant in a collection is in its rapid growth and freely produced flowers. It forms a globular body, a little taller than it is wide, about 4 inches in diameter, consisting of thirteen ribs with areoles situated on the tip of

HAMATOCACTUS SETISPINUS

small tubercles, about ½ inch apart. These areoles carry about fifteen straight, fine, spreading spines and one to three longer, stouter central spines which are curved back at the tip into a hook — a characteristic feature of this plant. The flowers are predominantly yellow; the inner petals are lance-shaped, yellow, reddish at the base; the outer petals greenish-yellow with reddish borders. The fruit when it appears is a magnificent red.

HELIOCEREUS SPECIOSUS

HELIOCEREUS speciosus. Central Mexico. This epiphytic plant lives in all the higher forested areas of Mexico and Central America. The younger parts of the stem are reddish, later becoming darker; they have three to five ribs bordered with areoles about 1 inch apart, from which arise six to eight spines about ½ inch long, yellowish at first, becoming slightly brownish. The beauty of this plant is in its diurnal flowers, with corollas 6–7 inches long, red with a metallic-blue sheen — a feature found only in cactus flowers. *Heliocereus speciosus* has been used in crosses with *Epiphyllum* species to obtain many of the beautiful varieties grown today. Unlike other cacti, this species needs a compost rich in leaf-mould.

HYLOCEREUS triangularis. Jamaica. This species was described as early as 1696, and is the longest known of the columnar cacti with triangular stems. It is a climber, and can also form dense clumps on the ground which are a magnificent sight when the plant flowers. The stem is triangular in section, shiny green, 1 – 1½ inches thick and up to 26 feet long. The areoles are surmounted by five to eight short, brown, stiff, straight spines. The ribs are almost straight, with only very slight undulations. The magnificent flower is nocturnal, lasting only one night; it is white, sometimes fragrant at a certain point in its development, and very large, with a long tube, and can grow to 1 foot or more in diameter. The fruit is edible, about the size of a turkey's egg. This plant should be trained on a frame, which needs to be large to allow the long stems to develop fully.

HYLOCEREUS TRIANGULARIS

LEMAIREOCEREUS pruinosus or **RITTEROCEREUS pruinosus.** Mexico. In its native habitat this species can attain a height of 16 – 23 feet, with upright or hanging branches; as a cultivated plant it has a single stem with five to seven clearly defined ribs, of a matt ashy-green with a whitish bloom appearing in arch-like bands. The areoles have five to seven spreading spines up to 1 inch long, and one stronger, brownish spine 1¼ inches long. The flowers are diurnal, about 3 inches long, with pink sep-

LEMAIREOCEREUS PRUINOSUS

als and white petals. The fruits are edible, and in Mexico are an important commercial crop. This species is not uncommonly cultivated in this country, but it grows to a much smaller size and the fruits hardly ever appear.

LOBIVIA chrysantha. Argentina. This cactus is globular but often irregular, measuring 2½ – 3 inches across. It has about thirteen ribs separated by deep grooves. The epidermis is light green. The areoles, set about ½ inch apart, produce a greyish wool when young and five to eight spines, all of them spreading, reddish with a black tip, later turning grey; the spines are widely spread, pointed, thin, straight and up to almost 1 inch long. The flower is slightly scented, and is a little smaller than that of *Lobivia aurea* which it otherwise closely resembles; it is only 2 inches long, with golden-yellow petals tinged with purple-red in the throat. This species

LOBIVIA CHRYSANTHA

is very popular with collectors because it flowers very freely. On the other hand, the plant gives off few suckers, and is usually propagated by seeds.

LOBIVIA famatimensis. This is a small species of *Lobivia*, usually with a single stem, but which can also form clumps by giving off

LOBIVIA FAMATIMENSIS

shoots. The body is oval or slightly elongate, up to 6 inches long at most and about 2 inches thick, with about fifteen shallow irregular ribs covered along their entire length with small tubercles. The areoles have numerous whitish or yellowish spreading spines ⅛ – ½ inch long, and one shorter central spine. All these spines are pectinate and cover the stem almost completely. The flowers, which arise on the upper part of the plant, are about 1½ inches long, yellow with a green pistil. There are numerous cultivated varieties which differ from the type in the coloration of their flowers, which varies from white to deep red and in the length of their spines. The name *Lobivia* is interesting in view of the fact that it is an anagram of Bolivia where these plants grow.

LOPHOPHORA williamsii (Peyotl). Mexico. A globular plant, wider than it is tall, about 3 inches in diameter, with a variable, yellowish-green epidermis. It has about eight shallow ribs separated by narrow grooves.

The areoles are woolly but have no spines. The flowers are small, 2 inches across, their colour ranging from white to pink; they appear at the centre of the plant and last several days. This is the most 'mysterious' cactus of the whole family. It contains a toxic alkaloid and is thought to be a sacred plant by some Mexican tribes, who call it the God Plant. The juice was drunk as a true remedy against all misfortunes. The taking of extracts of the plant produces fantastic, brilliantly coloured visual hallucinations. The collection of the cactus was the occasion for big annual ceremonies, and this custom is still practised in some parts of Mexico. The scientific study of the main active extracts of *Lophophora williamsii* has led to their use in modern medicine.

MALACOCARPUS leninghausii or **ECHINOCACTUS leninghausii.** Southern Brazil. This pale-green, cylindrical cactus grows to over 3 feet in height and 4 inches in diameter in its native habitat; in cultivation in our climate, a height of 20 inches when fully grown would be a good size. The plant body has about thirty narrow ribs bordered with close-set areoles, each of which gives rise to about fifteen slender, pale–yellow, spreading spines about $^1/_5$ inch long, and three or four golden-yellow

MALACOCARPUS LENINGHAUSII

central spines, which can reach a length of 1½ inches or more. Unusual features of this plant are its irregular growth, and its tip which always seems to lean to one side. The flowers appear at the top of the plant near the middle but only when it has reached a considerable size; they are 1½ – 2 inches long and slightly wider, with narrow petals generally of a golden-yellow colour. These flowers last for several days. This species is often grafted, but it can grow perfectly well on its own roots.

MAMILLARIA bocasana. Mexico. This *Mamillaria* is a dark bluish-green, small (1½ – 2 inches across), but forms fairly large clumps by successive generations of shoots. The numerous tubercles, which are a characteristic of the members of this group, are about ½ inch long, and in their axils they produce very short silky white hairs. The areoles, set at the tips of the tubercles, round or slightly oval in outline, carry numerous white, woolly, spreading spines nearly 1 inch long, and two to four central spines, coloured yellow or brown, one of which is always recurved into a hook at the tip. The flowers are small (about ⅔ inch), white to yellowish-white, veined with red on the inside of the petals, reddish on the outside. The abundant and long-lasting flowers of this cactus, which stand out vividly among the white hairs, make it very popular with collectors. It

MAMILLARIA BOCASANA

is easily propagated by cuttings, but to obtain good specimens it is advisable to let the plant give off shoots.

MAMILLARIA plumosa. Mexico. This plant looks rather like a small white cushion; it is formed by numerous shoots about 2 inches long and of the same thickness. The pale-green epidermis is completely hidden by the covering of about forty silky, feathery white spines which arise at the tip of each tubercle. The tubercles are cylindrical, about ½ inch long and up to ⅛ inch thick. The flowers are small, white and very fragrant; they appear only very rarely in our climate. This plant is usually propagated by grafts, because the roots cannot stand soil which is moist for any length of time and will eventually die in it. But if it is grown on its own roots it is possible to obtain specimens over 8 inches in diameter. These plants should be watered at long intervals in the summer, and not at all in the winter. Care must always be taken not to moisten the woolly covering, to prevent rotting. This species needs plenty of light.

MAMILLARIA PLUMOSA

MAMILLARIA prolifera. Southern United States. As its name indicates, this *Mamillaria* gives off abundant shoots. It produces huge clumps formed, as in the last species, by successive generations of small shoots about 1½ inches thick and up to 2 inches tall. It is almost completely hidden under its many spines; of these, twenty to thirty are bristly, white, spreading, and five to nine are central, yellow-tipped; the axils have long, white, silky-woolly hairs. The flowers are numerous, about ½ inch long, white tinged with pink or yellow. The fruits are red, rather elongated (about ½ inch long) and often curved; they last for a long time and are as decorative as the flowers. The numerous varieties of this species include *haitiensis*, which grows as freely as the type, with stronger stems, a distinctly bluish epidermis, and spines which mature to a pure white.

MAMILLARIA PROLIFERA

NOPALXOCHIA phyllantoides. Mexico. This plant was recorded as long ago as 1651 and bears its original Aztec name. The branches are cylindrical at the base, then become wide and flat like a crenate leaf, with a green or pale-green epidermis, often slightly reddish, with a prominent midrib. The flowers are 4 inches long, more or less bell-shaped, the outer petals wide open, lance-shaped, the inner petals lance-shaped, blunt, pink or pale red on the outer surface and paler on the inside. The plant can reach a height of over 3 feet and in spring produces abundant flowers which can last for up to three weeks. It should be grown in the same way as *Phyllocactus*, which it resembles in many features, and it is propagated by branch cuttings.

OPUNTIA bergeriana (Prickly Pear). Origin unknown. The joints of this plant, often incorrectly called leaves, are really modified branches; they are oval or somewhat elongate, pale green to greyish-green, 6–10 inches long. The areoles give rise to tiny yellow spines with brown bases, ¾ – 1½ inches long. This species flowers freely, producing numerous red flowers, later replaced by fruits which are also red when ripe. The fruits, known as Indian Figs, are most abundant on *Opuntia ficus indica*, which in Mexico is grown to produce them commercially.

OPUNTIA clavarioides or **AUSTROCYLINDROPUNTIA clavarioides.** Chile. The oddest of the Opuntias, with a very unusual appearance. It is a low plant with a somewhat shapeless tuberous root which gives off an underground stem about 4 inches long, on the end of which aerial roots develop. The joints are greenish-brown, sometimes in the form of an inverted truncated cone, sometimes cylindrical, growing in groups of four to six a little like the fingers of a hand; they cannot be confused with the joints of any other Opuntia. The epidermis is smooth and shiny, and the areoles look like big white spots; they grow very close together and

OPUNTIA CLAVARIOIDES

OPUNTIA mycrodasys. Mexico. This charming plant is much liked by collectors. The joints tend to spread out, but the plant can grow to a height of about 20 inches. The joints are flat, slightly oval or rounded, almost 4 inches across, coloured a brilliant green. The areoles, which are arranged regularly, have no spines but carry numerous yellow glochids, so dense that they form little cushions. The glochids are covered with barbed hooks and can lodge themselves in a finger, even if they are

are covered with short, white woolly hair and four to ten very small spines spread out against the epidermis of the stem. The flower is rare; it measures about 2 inches and is a rather vague, pale greenish-brown. The only way this species can be propagated under cultivation is by grafting.

OPUNTIA MICRODASY

just lightly touched, and are very hard to get out; the plant should be handled with great care, using gloves or some tool to hold it. The flower is either pure yellow or yellow and red; but rarely appears here. Two varieties which are worth mentioning are *alba*, with white glochids, and *rufida*, with reddish-brown glochids.

OPUNTIA subulata. Peru. Opuntias are divided into two groups according to the shape of their stems: Platyopuntias, with flat joints, and Cylindropuntias, with cylindrical stems. *Opuntia subulata* belongs to the second group. It forms bushes which can grow to a height of over 12 feet, with green cylindrical branches, the younger ones covered with white elongate tubercles on the tip of which are the areoles. The areoles give rise to a few yellowish glochids and one or two, rarely more, pale-

OPUNTIA SUBULATA

yellow, straight, rigid spines up to 3 inches in length. In addition, each areole also carries a green, semi-cylindrical, subulate, pointed leaf 4 – 5 inches long, which may persist for several years. This plant is readily propagated by cuttings, and is also used to take grafts of other species. It will not flower indoors.

OREOCEREUS CELSIANUS

OREOCEREUS celsianus. Bolivia. This is a very woolly columnar cactus which can reach a height of over 3 feet and about 4 inches in diameter; it branches near the base. The body consists of eight to seventeen slightly undulate ribs, with the woolly areoles carried on the swellings about ½ – ¾ inch apart. The areoles produce whitish silky hairs about 2 inches long which cover the plant almost entirely, ten yellowish-brown spreading spines up to 1 inch long, and one to four bigger central spines 3 inches long. This plant rarely flowers indoors, but it is nevertheless very attractive with its long spines growing through the mass of silky white hairs. It grows slowly and can stand low temperatures (40° F); in the Mediterranean region it is a hardy species.

OREOCEREUS trollii. Bolivia. This is generally rather similar to the last species. The stem is pale green, upright, growing to at most about 3 ft. in height, and in older plants gives off shoots at the base. The stems are thinner than in the species described above, reaching a diameter of only 2½ – 4 inches; they are formed by fifteen to twenty five undulate ribs bearing areoles about an inch apart, just above the swellings. The areoles give rise to a large num-

OREOCEREUS TROLLII

ber of woolly hairs 1–2 inches long, creamy-white to light grey, which soon become tangled and completely cover the plant. From this woolly coat there appear, on each areole, about ten more or less thick spreading spines approximately ¾ inch long, and one to three much stronger central spines up to 2 inches long, orange-red becoming yellow, which grow almost horizontally out from the stem. The flowers are pale red; they appear only on fully grown plants and are rarely seen indoors. This plant is easy to grow and can stand low temperatures; its natural habitat is at 12,000 – 15,000 feet above sea level.

PACHYCEREUS pringlei. California. In its natural habitat this is a huge plant, individuals attaining a height of 65 feet, with much-branched bodies over 3 feet thick. In our climate it grows with a single stem, green to dark green, to a diameter of about 8 inches. The stem consists of

PACHYCEREUS PRINGLEI

about twelve ribs separated by deep grooves. The areoles are large, with short, grey, woolly hairs, roughly twelve spreading spines and about eight central spines, two, three or four of which are stronger than the rest. The flower is diurnal, white, growing at the top of the stem, on the side, in a thick patch of hairs which appear before the flowers. In California, the flowers and unripe fruits are used as cattle-fodder in times of drought. The pulp of the fruit can be prepared as a jam, and is also used as a treatment for dysentery.

PARODIA chrysacanthion. Argentina. The body of this cactus is about 2 – 2½ inches across, usually globular, sometimes becoming semi-globular with age. It has 24 ribs arranged in spirals, consisting of small tubercles, each about ¼ inch long, with an areole on the tip. The areole gives rise to thirty to forty thin yellow woolly hairs, sharp spreading spines nearly 1 inch long, and one slightly stronger central spine. These spines are very bright, golden-yellow at first becoming brown later. The flowers, about ¾ inch long, also golden-yellow, appear on the upper part of the areoles in the centre of the plant. This attractive species is easy to grow, particularly when it is produced from a graft.

PARODIA aureispina. Argentina. The spreading spines of this species are white and the five or six central spines golden-yellow, the lowest forming a hook at the tip.

PARODIA
CHRYSACANTHION

PARODIA
AUREISPINA

PARODIA SANGUINIFLORA

PARODIA sanguiniflora. Argentina. This species is the same size as *Parodia chrysacanthion*, with a single, globular stem coloured a delicate green, woolly at the top. The ribs are similarly arranged in spirals, with small conical tubercles bearing areoles ¼ inch apart. When young, each areole is covered with woolly hairs, and also gives rise to about fifteen fine, white spreading spines about ¼ inch long, and four brownish central spines arranged in a cross, the lowest of which is about ¾ inch long and hooked at the tip. An outstanding feature of this species is its blood-red flowers, 1½ inches across, which grow like a bouquet from the top of the plant.

PARODIA maassii. Argentina, Bolivia. The flowers of this species are brick-red, and the central spines are light brown, curved.

All the Parodias flower freely.

PARODIA
MAASSII

PERESKIA aculeata (Barbados Gooseberry). Argentina, Paraguay. The genus *Pereskia* forms an intermediate stage between the leafed plants

PERESKIA ACULEATA

and the cacti. They look just like dicotyledons, and can only be identified by the similarities they have botanically to the cacti. The branches are not jointed and the areoles have no glochids. The flowers are stalked. *Pereskia aculeata* was introduced in Europe in 1696. It is a bushy shrub with green sarmentous branches, bearing areoles with only two or three spines. The leaves are 2 – 4 inches long, flat, oval, acuminate, only slightly fleshy, coloured slate below and a brilliant green above; they are caducous. The flowers are pinkish white, measuring 1 – 1½ inches, and very fragrant; they appear in the autumn. *Pereskia* is sometimes grown as a botanical curiosity, but mainly it is used to take grafts. It is freely propagated by cuttings.

PHYLLOCACTUS hybrides. These are magnificent plants, especially at flowering time, characterized by branches flattened into the form of leaves, branched at the base, crenate, with the areole in the concave part of the margin. In the natural state they live as epiphytes, like *Epiphyllum* which has already been described, which indicates the way they must be cultivated: they require a light, rich leaf-mould, moisture, warmth and

PHYLLOCACTUS HYBRIDES

subdued light, and reduced watering after the flowers have appeared. These plants have been selected, crossed originally with *Heliocereus speciosus*, then recrossed among themselves; in America they are the object of numerous horticultural competitions. The flowers are usually large, 8 – 10 inches across, and exist in various shades of every colour except blue; on good specimens several hundred blooms can appear at the same time.

REBUTIA minuscula. South America. This little cactus is fully grown when it reaches a height of 1½ inches and a diameter of ¼ – 1 inch, sometimes less. It is globular, slightly flattened on top, with a green or pale-green epidermis. It flowers very freely, and each year gives off a number of small shoots at the base. It has no ribs, but is covered with small round or hexagonal tubercles arranged in about twenty spiral rows, bearing areoles on their tips. The areoles carry

REBUTIA MINUSCULA

twenty to twenty five small whitish or yellowish spines. In spring, numerous red flowers, 1½ inches long and about ¾ inch across, appear all around the base of the plant; these flowers close in the evening, then the next morning open out again, staying open for several days. This is an easy plant to cultivate, growing equally well in partial shade and in full sunshine, and it is a favourite with all collectors.

REBUTIA pseudodeminuta. Northern Argentina. This *Rebutia* grows in the natural state at an altitude of about 8,000 feet. It is globular, slightly flattened on top, with a diameter of about 2 – 2½ inches, sometimes more. It produces quite a lot of suckers at the base, which can be used for propagating the plant. The small areoles are set on the tip of tubercles arranged in spiral rows as in the last species. They carry eleven spreading spines about ¼ inch long, one of which points upwards, while the other, lower spines are shorter, white at the base and brownish towards the tip; the smallest are about ¼ inch long, the largest about ½ inch. The flowers appear at the base of the tubercles; they are

REBUTIA PSEUDODEMINUTA

just over 1 inch across, a brilliant red powdered with gold. *Rebutia pseudodeminuta* is a very attractive little plant which is easy to grow; it belongs to a genus which flowers very abundantly and in which young plants also flower, often disappearing completely under the mass of blooms.

REBUTIA senilis. Argentina. Generally very similar to the last two species, *Rebutia senilis* differs in its spines and in the colour of its flowers. The spines, numbering twenty five to thirty, glassy white with a yellow point, are all about the same size, reaching a length of ¾ – 1¼ inches. The flower appears at the base of the plant; it is wider than it is long (1¼ and 1½ inches respectively), coloured a pale carmine. This plant is very variable in its spines and in the colour of its flowers. Some of the varieties include: *iseliniana*, with a light-orange flower, *lilacinorosea*, which is lilac-pink, *kesselringiana*, which is yellow. The most remarkable is *semperflorens*, which has flowers growing in all the areoles.

REBUTIA SENILIS

RHIPSALIS cassutha. Southern Brazil. This species has long cylindrical stems which grow in the form of a pendulous clump reaching a height of several feet. It branches very abundantly, because each joint, which can reach a length of 1 foot or more, always gives rise to several more joints at its tip. The areoles are small and carry one or two very short white spines when they are young. The flowers are small, hardly ¼

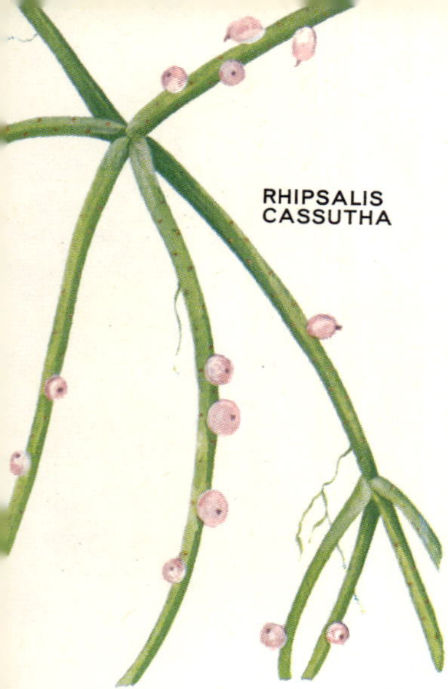

RHIPSALIS CASSUTHA

inch long; the petals are wide open, the outer ones triangular, green, slightly fleshy, the inner ones white to yellowish-white. The fruit is globular, small (less than ¼ inch across), white or pinkish-white, rather like the fruit of the mistletoe. Like so many cacti, this plant comes from America, but it is also the only species which has a quite separate place of origin in Africa and Ceylon. It may have been carried from one place to another by birds.

RHIPSALIS houlletiana. Brazil. This species has curiously shaped branches which form pendulous clumps 5 feet or more in length. They are very variable, growing either as long, thin cylindrical stems, or as narrow lamellae with a toothed margin, each up to 2 inches wide and about 16 – 20 inches long, narrowing slightly at the top where it joins the next similar segment. These flattened stems look like leaves and have a thick central vein. Often both

RHIPSALIS HOULLETIANA

types of branches appear on the same stem, looking rather like leaves carried on long stalks. The numerous small yellow flowers appear at the beginning of spring, on the concave part of the toothed margin of the flat branches. They are replaced by long-lasting globular red fruits. *Rhipsalis houlletiana* is particularly suitable for use as a hanging plant, because of the way its branches grow.

RHIPSALIS PACHYPTERA

RHIPSALIS pachyptera. Brazil. This species looks very much like a *Phyllocactus*; it is sturdy, with a bushy upright stem which can grow to a height of over 3 feet, and with big branches. The lower branches are divided into three elongate wings, which widen out into thick leaves, 3–8 inches long and 2–5 inches wide. The thick veins form, with the margins, rounded lobes with woolly areoles on the concave parts; the areoles have no spines. The epidermis is green, but the terminal joints often have purple-red margins. The flowers are about ½ inch long and grow on the marginal areoles. They are coloured pale yellow and are very short-lived. The persistent red fruits add to the decorative effect of the plant.

SCHLUMBERGERA gaertneri or **EPIPHYLLOPSIS gaertneri** (Easter Cactus). Southern Brazil. This very attractive plant is generally very similar in appearance to *Epiphyllum*, which was described earlier; in addition, it shares the same habitat and has similar requirements. The difference is in the shape of the joints and flowers, and in the flowering time. The joints are 1½ – 2 inches long, sometimes more, and up to 1 inch across. They are truncated at the tip and carry long silky hairs. The flowers are regular, 1½ – 2 inches long, violet-red, with petals arranged like a star. The flowers appear in spring, at Easter. When in bud, these plants cannot stand a change of environment and should be left in the same place as soon as the flower buds appear, otherwise these may drop off.

SELENICEREUS grandiflorus (Queen of the Night). Cuba, Jamaica. The stem of this columnar cactus may be creeping or climbing, growing to a length of several yards. It is yellowish green, about 1 inch in diameter, with five to seven indistinct branched ribs. The areoles are spaced about ½ inch apart, and carry seven to eleven slender yellowish spines ¼ inch long growing among silky hairs. The flower buds grow only on the latest year's stems. They appear in May-June, and the corolla opens a

SELENICEREUS GRANDIFLORUS

month later. The flowers are magnificent, and can readily attain a size of 8 – 12 inches. This huge flower has pure white petals, surrounded by a halo of very long orange sepals; it gives off a pleasant scent of vanilla, but it opens at dusk and lasts for only a few hours. The plant should be trained on a frame, and can be used to decorate verandas.

SELENICEREUS hamatus. Mexico. The trailing or climbing stems of this plant are about ¾ inch in diameter and can reach a length of 40 feet. They are light green and in the natural state send out a few aerial roots. These stems usually have four ribs, with characteristic beak-like enlargements below the areoles. Each areole has five or six silky spines about ¼ inch long, and two or three other, strong brown spines. The appearance of the flowers is spread out from the summer through to the autumn. They do not appear very frequently, but when they do they are very large, the biggest of the whole family, growing to 8 – 12 inches in diameter and 10 – 16 inches in length. The corolla of the flower is covered with long green sepals, and the petals themselves are an attractive milky white. The flowers open at dusk. To obtain the best effect from this plant, it should be trained on a large surface, so that it is very suitable for decorating verandas, for example.

SELENICEREUS HAMATUS

SETICEREUS icosagonus. Peru. This is an upright species, branched at the base, with a stem reaching 5 feet in height (but rarely more than 20 inches when cultivated in our climate) and 1 – 1½ inches in diameter. The epidermis is light green, and has fifteen to twenty narrow, rounded ribs. The areoles are oval, yellowish-white, set about ½ inch apart; they give rise to about thirty light-yellow spreading spines ½ inch long, and six to eight thicker central spines, ¾ inch long, light yellow to brownish-yellow in colour. The flowers are orange-red or red, about 3 inches long; they are tubular and open out only slightly at the tip. This species is often grafted on *Trichocereus spachianus*, but it also grows very well on its own roots.

TRICHOCEREUS spachianus. Argentina. This is a columnar cactus with an upright stem which can grow to a height of 5 ft. and a diameter of 1½ – 2½ inches. The epidermis is a brilliant pale green. In older plants, the stem is branched at the base and

TRICHOCEREUS SPACHIANUS

SETICEREUS ICOSAGONUS

has ten to fifteen blunt rounded ribs. The areoles are about ½ inch apart and carry eight to ten spreading spines about ½ inch long, and one slightly longer and thicker central spine. All these spines are yellow at first, becoming brown with age. Numerous flowers appear towards the top ot the stems, but only on fully grown plants. They measure about 8 inches, with long corollas,the outer petals greenish and the inner ones white. The flower is nocturnal, but stays open for part of the following morning, perhaps longer if it is shaded from the sunlight. This plant grows well, but tends to suffer in soil containing too much lime; it is also much better for the plant to water it with rainwater only, if this is possible.

COMMELINACEAE

TRADESCANTIA navicularis. Peru. The stems of this plant are thick and succulent, with very short internodes; they carry numerous thick leaves, which are strongly flattened on the midrib on the upper surface and keeled on the lower side. When the plant is

TRADESCANTIA NAVICULARIS

raised under favourable conditions, the leaves grow very close and seem to fit together. To prevent the stems from wilting, this plant must have good light, fresh air during the summer months, and during the winter should be kept at 45 – 50° F and watered very sparingly. It requires a free-draining compost and is propagated from cuttings. *Tradescantia albiflora* and *Tradescantia fluminensis*, both known as Wandering Jew, are very popular trailing plants which tolerate room conditions extremely well. They are easily propagated from stem cuttings during the summer months.

COTYLEDON ORBICULATA

CRASSULACEAE

COTYLEDON orbiculata. Southern Africa. This plant is as yet not very popular, although it is quite hardy and deserves to be more widely grown. It forms a bush with thick branching stems, upright or hanging, and can reach a height of 20 – 24 inches. The leaves are very short-stalked, oval, thick, glaucous, with a red band round the margin. The flowers are tubular, reddish, growing on a velvety stem 12 – 16 inches long; they appear in the summer. This plant needs air, plenty of light and frequent watering during the warm months, although it can stand being left without water for a short time. In summer, it can be placed on a balcony; in winter it should be put in a spot where the temperature is constant at about 50° F. During this period, watering should be considerably reduced. It can be propagated easily by branch or leaf cuttings.

COTYLEDON UNDULATA

COTYLEDON undulata. South Africa. This plant is without doubt the most beautiful of its genus. As a young plant it generally has a single stem 8 – 12 inches tall; as it grows older, the stem branches and can reach a height of 20 – 24 inches. The leaves are very decorative; they are 2 inches or more across, oval, spatulate at the base, with undulate margins, and completely covered with a white bloom. This species is more delicate than the last and should always be placed in strong light, otherwise it wilts and loses its leaves. It should be remembered that, generally speaking, all plants covered with a bloom or with downy hairs require as much light as possible. The flowers are reddish, tubular, arranged in a terminal cyme; they appear in the summer, but this plant rarely flowers indoors. This species needs plenty of air and in summer can be stood outdoors. In winter it needs a temperature of 50 – 55° F.

CRASSULA arborescens. South Africa. This plant forms bushes of thick, succulent, much-branched stems, which can reach a height of 2½ – 3½ feet. The leaves are about 2 inches wide, oval, rounded, thick; they have a purple margin and the upper surface is covered with small reddish dots. There are several other species, with a gen-

CRASSULA
ARBORESCENS

erally similar appearance, which can be grown as indoor plants.

CRASSULA argentea. Cape Province. This species has shining, oblong leaves, sometimes with red margins.

CRASSULA
ARGENTEA

CRASSULA lactea. South Africa. This species forms smaller plants, with greyish-green leaves dotted with white above. It flowers more freely than the last two species, the flowers appearing in autumn; they are white, and give off a slight scent of vanilla. All these plants need good

CRASSULA
LACTEA

light and plenty of air, so that they can be put in the open air during the summer months; in winter, they should be put in a situation with plenty of light, at a temperature of 50 – 55° F.

CRASSULA falcata. South-eastern Cape Province. In its native habitat, this *Crassula* can grow to a height of 3 – 8 feet. When cultivated in our climate, in a pot, it can be considered fully grown when it reaches a height of 20 – 24 inches. This species is liked for its unusual leaves, which are 3 – 4 inches long and 1 – 1½ inches wide, fleshy, and coloured grey-green; they grow in opposite, intersecting pairs, the lower leaves being curiously curved into the shape of a sickle blade, the upper ones gradually becoming smaller and less curved. The plant also has a very attractive inflorescence, consisting of a corymb of small (½ inch) but very numerous bright crimson flowers. The plant flowers quite often indoors, opening between June and September and lasting sometimes for almost a month. This plant can be grown easily in a light soil, like that used for cacti: one third leafmould, one third garden soil and one third river sand. In winter, *Crassula falcata* requires a temperature of 50 – 55° F and good light.

CRASSULA FALCATA

CRASSULA lycopodioides. Southern Africa. This species is very different from the other Crassulas; it grows no longer than 6 – 8 inches, with slender stems, often procumbent at the base, with the tips growing upright. The leaves are small, oval, pointed, imbricate, arranged round the stem in four rows. The flowers are very small and appear in the leaf

ECHEVERIA AGAVOIDES

axils. The variety *monstruosa* has small, stunted-looking branches growing from the axils, which form thicker stems than in the type. Another variety, *variegata*, has light-green leaves with a yellowish-white tinge; this plant grows less vigorously. It forms dense clumps, with the branches drooping over the side of the pot, which makes it very suitable as a hanging plant. This species is propagated very easily by cuttings, and by separating off the branches which lie on the surface of the soil and take root. It is very hardy indoors, and in winter it requires more frequent watering than the thick-leaved Crassulas.

ECHEVERIA agavoides. Mexico. The leaves of this species are arranged in a tight stemless rosette. They are oval, triangular in cross-section, 2½ – 3 inches long, yellowish-green, terminating in a point which is usually coloured red. The inflorescence is about 1 foot long, with reddish flowers with yellow lobes. *Cristata* has a rather shapeless rosette and is perhaps the least elegant of the vari-

CRASSULA LYCOPODIOIDES

eties, but it has a definite advantage as regards propagation: while the type produces few suckers, this variety freely gives off normal offsets which can simply be separated off as cuttings; these offsets readily take root. This species is very hardy, and requires light and plenty of air. During the winter, it requires a temperature of 45 – 50° F and should be watered with extreme care.

ECHEVERIA secunda. This species is the hardiest of all the genus. The leaves are oval, glaucous green, covered with a whitish bloom; they are 2½ – 3 inches long and form a rosette which in the young plant is stemless, but in older plants is carried on a short fleshy stem. The plant gives off numerous offsets which can be used to propagate it. It needs a sunny situation and plenty of air to prevent wilting, and it is advisable to put it on a window-sill or balcony during the summer months. In winter it must have a temperature of 40 – 45° F and a situation with good light. The flowers are orange-red; they form an inflorescence which is recurved at the tip, and appear between June and August. Each rosette pro-

ECHEVERIA
SECUNDA

duces several flower-stems. This plant is still widely used in carpet bedding. It requires a moderate level of humidity throughout the year and can stand being left without watering for some time.

KALANCHOE tubiflora. Madagascar. The leaves of this plant are cylindrical, shining green with purple spots, 2 – 3 inches long and 1 – 1½ inches wide, bearing buds at the tip. The flowers are large, pendent, with a bright red corolla. The stems of this species lose their leaves after flowering, so that it is preferable to grow new plants each year.

KALANCHOE globulifera. Madagascar. These plants require a great deal of light and are not often used for permanent indoor decoration. They do, however, flower very freely and form very attractive plants suitable for temporary decoration. *Kalanchoe globulifera* is much-branched, with oval, spatulate, glabrous leaves carried on short stalks; they are coloured a brilliant green, and the margins have widely spaced, rounded teeth. A stalk carrying red flowers grows from the tip of each main stem. The variety *coccinea*, also called *Kalanchoe blossfeldiana*, is a more compact plant with brilliant red flowers. This species requires a temperature of 55 – 60° F and a situation with good light is essential. After flowering the plant starts to wither and it is then very difficult to keep it alive indoors. These plants are widely grown commercially, and they have been selected and crossed to obtain varieties with larger inflorescences, coloured differently in various shades of red and yellow.

KALANCHOE tomentosa. Madagascar. This species has very decorative leaves, and is undoubtedly the hardiest of the genus, as long as it is assured plenty of light, a temperature of 55–60° F during the winter months,

KALANCHOE TOMENTOSA

and only moderate amounts of water; the soil must not, however, be allowed to dry up completely. The stems are branched and carry thick, elongate, oval leaves, 2–3 inches long, which are completely covered on both surfaces with white down which contrasts with the rest of the plant. The flowers are pale mauve and grow in a terminal spike; however, they are only of secondary interest, as this species rarely flowers indoors. Propagation is by stem or leaf cuttings.

PACHYPHYTUM oviferum. Mexico. This little plant is almost bushlike, with short stems and a varying number of branches. The leaves are a pale grey-green, ¾–1½ inches long and ¾–1 inch wide, very thick, oval, curiously pill-shaped, and growing very close together almost in a rosette. The most attractive feature of the plant is the white bloom which covers it almost entirely; to preserve this bloom, care must be taken not to get it wet. The flowers are red, bell-shaped, and grow in clusters on short stalks;

PACHYPHYTUM OVIFERUM

they generally appear in May. This plant can be propagated very easily by offsets, or better still by leaf cuttings. In winter, it should get a temperature of 50 – 55° F, good light and a moderate amount of water.

SEDUM rubrotinctum. Mexico. This is a small shrub growing to a height of 4 – 8 inches. The branches are up to ⅛ inch in diameter, fleshy when young, later becoming woody; they are creeping at first, then upright. The cylindrical leaves are arranged alternately all along the stem, forming a rosette at the tip. The plant is grown mainly for these attractive fleshy leaves, $^1/_5$ inch thick and ¾ inch long, which are a brilliant green with reddish-brown tips, the shade varying with the amount of sunlight the plant gets. If it is kept dry, this species can stand quite a lot of cold, but it is better not to subject it to low temperatures. The flower is a brilliant yellow. The variety *roseum* has leaves which are completely pink, becoming more or less dark depending again on the amount of sunlight.

SEDUM RUBROTINCTUM

SEMPERVIVUM arachnoideum (Cobweb House-leek). Europe. Strictly speaking this is not an indoor plant, because it is a perfectly hardy species which passes the European winter in the open. The numer-

SEMPERVIVUM
ARACHNOIDEUM

ous small leaves form a stemless rosette. Each leaf terminates in a long, silky white hair, and these hairs intermingle and cover the rosette with what looks like a spider's web. The plant gives off numerous offsets, which surround it and form a large clump entirely covered with the threads. It does not like the dry air of houses and flats, and it is advisable to put the plant on a window-sill or on a sunny balcony. The flowers are bright red and grow in a spike; they appear in June. This species can be propagated very easily by separating the offsets.

EUPHORBIACEAE

EUPHORBIA canariensis. Canary Islands. The different genera of this family take very varied forms, and even within this genus, *Euphorbia*, many of the species differ widely from each other. The species *canariensis* forms clumps branched at the base; the branches are greyish-green, usually four-sided, sometimes with up to six sides, with small black spines about $^1/_5$ inch long growing in pairs on each angle.

EUPHORBIA
CANARIENSIS

EUPHORBIA resinifera. Morocco. This species forms very compact clumps up to 20 inches tall. The branches are greyish-green, four-sided, with greyish spines $^1/_5$ – $^1/_4$ inch long, growing in pairs on the angles. In the axils of the spines grow small yellow flowers which open in the summer.
If they are cut, all Euphorbias give out a white latex, which is caustic and dangerous.

EUPHORBIA RESINIFERA

EUPHORBIA meloformis. South Africa. This species is very different from the last two described, growing in the form of a ribbed sphere.

EUPHORBIA MELOFORMIS

The eight to ten ribs are green, generally marbled with brown if the plant is exposed to sunlight. It never has leaves. The flowers are small and not very decorative, and grow on a stalk 1-1½ inches long. When the flowers fall, the stalks become dried and persist on the plant for several months. The plant often produces offsets at the base, which can be left grouped round the plant to form a clump, or separated off to propagate it.

EUPHORBIA obesa. Cape Province. This species, less widespread than the last, has rather shallow ribs. It looks like a little green sphere with oblique reddish stripes on each rib. The plant does not give off suckers and can be propagated only by seeds, which are difficult to obtain as this species is dioecious.

EUPHORBIA splendens. Madagascar. In its native habitat, this is a shrub growing to a height of 3 – 6 feet. or more; cultivated in a pot, it forms plants 30 – 40 inches tall. The branches are greyish, four-sided, with numerous spines ½ - ¾ inch long. The leaves are 2½ – 3 inches long, oval, green on both surfaces; during the winter they yellow and fall. The flowers are arranged in an umbel on a stalk 3 – 4 inches long; they are small, but are accompanied by two red bracts and are very decorative and long-lasting. The variety *mainiana* is identical except that it has yellow bracts. *Euphorbia splendens* is a sturdy plant which flowers freely if it is given plenty of light. In winter it should be watered only moderately. It is propagated, preferably in June, by stem cuttings, the cut ends of which should be allowed to dry for several days before inserting in a sandy mixture. The cuttings should be watered very sparingly until they form roots.

EUPHORBIA SPLENDENS

LILIACEAE

ALOE arborescens. South Africa. In its native habitat this species forms a stem which can grow to a height of 12 – 16 feet; in our part of the world it grows no higher than about 3 feet. The leaves are 16 – 20 inches long, linear, lance-shaped, glaucous, with a border of soft spines. Older leaves gradually droop, become dried, and lie against the stem.

ALOE ciliaris. Cape Province. The stem of this species is slender, sarmentous, and carries alternative, linear, lance-shaped leaves, green bordered with white teeth.

ALOE CILIARIS

ALOE MITRIFORMIS

ALOE mitriformis. Cape Province. This species has a stem up to 3 feet long, carrying, usually along its whole length, oval, lance-shaped, incurved leaves with a toothed margin. There are more soft teeth on the under surface of the leaf, at the tip.

These plants freely give off shoots at the base, which can be effectively used as cuttings.

ALOE aristata. South Africa. Many people confuse aloes and agaves. Aloes have soft, thick, succulent leaves bordered with soft spines; the central leaves are open from the time they first appear. The agaves have stiff, thick, fibrous leaves bordered with hard spines and tipped with a sharp point; their young leaves are rolled up into a cone at the centre of the rosette. The inflorescence of the aloes grows from the axils, while that of the agaves is terminal. *Aloe aristata* forms a stemless rosette of dark grey-green leaves. These leaves are 3–4 inches long, widened at the top, narrow at the tip, bordered with soft whitish teeth and tipped with a long silky awn. The lower surface is covered with small white tubercles arranged roughly in transverse lines. The flowers are orange-red and grow in an inflorescence 12–14 inches tall. This species can be propagated by leaf cuttings or by the suckers that the plant sometimes produces.

ALOE plicatilis. South Africa. Almost all the species of aloes have leaves arranged in a more or less dense rosette, or inserted along a large part of the stem, but *Aloe plicatilis* has a rather dif-

ALOE PLICATILIS

ferent, characteristic habit. The stems branch dichotomously and carry the leaves at their tips. These leaves are soft, linear, rounded at the tip, glaucous green, with a narrow white margin which is finely toothed in the upper part of the leaf; they are distichous and form a fan. This is a slow-growing species, having only one stem in the young plant; it is only in older plants that the characteristic appearance develops. *Aloe plicatilis* does not produce suckers and it is much more difficult to get stem cuttings to strike, compared with other species. The plant rarely flowers indoors.

ALOE variegata (Partridge-breasted Aloe). South Africa. This plant is generally stemless or with a very short stalk. The leaves are thick, triangular in section, 4–8 inches long, imbricate, inserted in three ranks. The upper surface of the leaves is marked by a wide groove, the lower surface is keeled. They are dark green with white transverse stripes and a narrow white border. The flowers are tubular, red, forming simple clusters 12 - 14 inches tall. This species cannot stand direct sunshine, or too

ALOE VARIEGAT[A]

much moisture during the winter. Care should be taken not to allow drops of water to fall into the centre of the plant, to avoid the danger of rotting. Propagation is by separation of the offsets.

GASTERIA nigricans. Cape Province. This plant has a very short stem, carrying distichous, thick, tongue-

GASTERIA NIGRICANS

HAWORTHIA FASCIATA

shaped leaves, 6–8 inches long, dark green with white spots. The flowers are tubular, inflated at the base, coloured orange-pink; they are pendent and grow in an inflorescence 24–32 inches long.

GASTERIA verrucosa. Cape Province. The leaves of this species are also green, distichous, but are 4–6 inches long, with truncate margins, concave on the upper surface, and covered with whitish tubercles which give them a granular appearance. The inflorescence is unbranched, 16–20 inches tall, with pendent red and green flowers. These plants can be propagated by detaching the offsets that they produce, or by taking leaf cuttings.

HAWORTHIA fasciata. Cape Province. This is a stemless plant with numerous leaves about 3 inches long arranged in a rosette. These leaves are flat and dark green above, convex on the lower surface, which is marked with white transverse lines made up of small white tubercles growing very close together. Several other species with a very similar appearance are also used for decorative purposes.

HAWORTHIA margaritifera. Cape Province. The leaves of this species are dotted with irregularly spaced white tubercles, which are more numerous on the lower surface.

GASTERIA VERRUCOSA

HAWORTHIA attenuata. Cape Province. This plant also has leaves covered with white tubercles, arranged in transverse lines, which are more numerous on the lower surface.

All these species flower freely indoors. The flowers are white with green stripes, and grow in a slender inflorescence 12–16 inches long. These plants are all propagated by division of offsets.

HAWORTHIA reinwardtii. Cape Province. This Haworthia has a very different appearance from the species described above, forming stems 6 – 8 inches in length entirely covered with small leaves. These leaves are triangular, 2–2½ inches long and about ½ inch wide at the base, and are inserted on the stem in a spiral. They are green, slightly concave above, the lower surface being convex and bearing numerous small greenish-white tubercles on fine longitudinal ribs.

HAWORTHIA REINWARDTII

HAWORTHIA VISCOSA

HAWORTHIA viscosa. Cape Province. This species has dark-green, rugose, imbricate leaves, growing the whole length of the stem in three vertical or slightly spiral lines.

All these species freely produce offsets, forming attractive clumps. Propagation is very simple: the offsets are detached and planted out in pots; successful striking is assured every time. These plants like situations with good light. In winter, waterings should be reduced to avoid rotting the roots.

NOLINA recurvata (Bottle Tree). Mexico. This plant has a single stem with an almost cylindrical enlargement at the base; in a healthy plant this can attain a diameter of 8 – 12 inches, giving the stem a bottle like appearance which has earned the plant its popular name. The leaves are narrow, linear, leathery, but gracefully recurved; they grow in a group at the top of the stem. This is a fairly sturdy plant which does well indoors and prefers a temperature of 45 – 50° F. For this reason it is often used to decorate rooms where there is little heating. It should be placed preferably in a situation with plenty of light. In summer, it can be put out of doors, and can be left without watering for several days with no harm done. In winter, it should be watered sparingly. This species has become naturalized in the Mediterranean region, where it is grown to good effect in gardens. It never flowers indoors.

NOLINA RECURVATA

PORTULACAEAE

ANACAMPSEROS. South Africa. This genus consists of several species, some of which do well in indoor cultivation and are currently very popular. *Anacampseros*

ANACAMPSEROS TELEPHIASTRUM

telephiastrum forms small branched clumps, 3–4 inches high, with oval, green leaves, glabrous but with short, white hairs at the base. The flowers are small, reddish, and grow in clusters. *Anacampseros rufescens* grows shorter (¾ inch), oval leaves, matt green above, reddish on the under surface, with numerous wavy hairs. The red flowers appear in July-August. These plants can be put outside in the summer months, and in winter can be kept at 40–45° F if they are kept almost dry. They are propagated easily by cuttings.

PORTULACARIA

afra. South Africa. This is an attractive little shrub which grows no taller than about 3 feet when cultivated in a pot. It is much-branched, with fleshy red stems and thick persistent, obovate, rounded leaves about ½ inch wide. It looks a little like the Japanese dwarf trees which are again becoming very popular. It is

PORTULACARIA AFRA

a very decorative species, even as a young plant. There is a very elegant variety with leaves variegated with white, which is just as suitable for indoor cultivation as this type. *Portulacaria afra* requires a situation with good light, and during the summer months plenty of air. In winter, it can be kept at a temperature of 50–54° F, with light watering. It is a slow-growing species which can be propagated easily by branch cuttings in May-June. The small pink flowers rarely appear on plants grown indoors.

VITACEAE

CISSUS quadrangularis. Tropical Africa and Asia. A climbing plant belonging to the same family as the grape-vine, but with a very different appearance. The stems are green, four-sided, with slightly undulate angles; at each node they give rise to a small, fleshy, three-lobed leaf. There is usually a tendril growing opposite each leaf, by which the stem hangs on to its support. The plant should be trained on a frame. In winter, it requires a temperature of 45–50° F and should be watered less frequently; it enters a semi-resting state after the leaves have fallen. This species can be propagated easily by stem cuttings, which should be inserted in a light sandy compost.

CISSUS CACTIFORMIS

CISSUS cactiformis. East Africa. This plant has thicker stems than the last species. The four angles of the stem are sharper, very wavy, with a horny appearance. The leaves are caducous, oval, heart-shaped.

CISSUS QUADRANGULARIS

GLOSSARY

ACUMINATE: With long sharp tips.
ADVENTITIOUS: Roots etc. which are formed from an unusual position on the plant, sometimes accidental.
ANNULATED: With ring-like structures or characteristics.
AREOLE: A small cavity in which the spines arise, as in cacti.
AXIL: The cleft formed between the stem or axis of a plant and a leaf or branch.

BIFID: Forked, divided into two parts.
BIPINNATE: Having similar parts arranged opposite each other, as in a feather or leaf pinnate, these parts also opposite each other as in some ferns.
BRACTS: Scale-like supporting leaf.

CADUCOUS: With parts that fall off at an early stage.
CALYX: The outer floral leaves, the sepals are usually green, but sometimes coloured.
CLADODE: A branch arising from a leaf axil, or a stem resembling a leaf.
COROLLA: The inner whorl of flower leaves.
CORYMB: An inflorescence forming a flat-topped cluster of flowers.
CRENATE: Scalloped.
CYME: An inflorescence on a primary stem, bearing a single flower at the top which develops first, other flowers developing at later stages.

DENTATE: Toothed.
DIGITATE: With leaves or other parts arranged like the fingers of a hand.
DISTICHOUS: Arranged alternately so that the first leaf is directly under the third leaf.
DIURNAL: A flower which opens during the day and closes by night.

EPIDERMIS: A skin or outer layer.

GLABROUS: Without hairs.
GLAUCOUS: With green-blue surface bloom.
GLOCHID: Hairs with barbs, like arrow heads.

HASTATE: Spear shaped.

IMBRICATE: Bud scales, bracts or similar having parts overlapping.
INFLEXED: Bent downwards.
INFLORESCENCE: A stem bearing flowers.

LAMINA: A leaf layer, or blade of a leaf.

NODE: A joint or knob in a stem which normally bears leaves.

PALMATE: Divided into many lobes from a common centre.
PANICLE: A flower cluster the branches of which form a pyramid.
PECTINATE: Comblike.
PHOTOSYNTHESIS: The process by which a plant uses carbon dioxide, water and inorganic salts with sunlight and chlorophyll to build up into carbohydrates.
PINNULE: A secondary leaf on a pinnate or bipinnate leaf.
PISTIL: The organ of a flower which bears the ovule or seeds.

PROCUMBENT: Lying along the ground.

RACHIS: A stem or main axis of a leaf or flower.
RHIZOME: A stem running along the ground sending out roots into the ground and shoots above ground.
RUGASE: With wrinkles or ridges.

SEPAL: Each individual leaf of the floral part of the Calyx.
SORI: A mass of reproductive cells on a lower plant.
SORMENTUM: A stem of a climbing or running plant.
SPADIX: A flower with a fleshy or thickened stem usually supported by a spathe.
SPATHE: A large leaf enveloping and protecting a spadix.
SPATULATE: Spoon shaped.
STAMEN: The organ of the flower which bears pollen.
STIPE: A stalk as in mushrooms or seaweeds.
STOLON: A long shoot or branch which sometimes takes root at the tip and develops into a new plant.
SUBULATE: Narrow and tapering to a fine point.
SUCKER: A branch growing through the planting medium, becoming aerial and often forming an independent plant.

TENDRIL: A stem modified into a thin sensitive organ for attaching a plant to a surface and assisting a plant to climb.
TUBERCLES: Nodules or swellings on the roots of some plants.

UMBEL: Inflorescence in the form of a cluster.

INDEX